Palgrave Macmillan Studies in Banking and Financial Institutions

Series Editor
Philip Molyneux
University of Sharjah
Sharjah, United Arab Emirates

The Palgrave Macmillan Studies in Banking and Financial Institutions series is international in orientation and includes studies of banking systems in particular countries or regions as well as contemporary themes such as Islamic Banking, Financial Exclusion, Mergers and Acquisitions, Risk Management, and IT in Banking. The books focus on research and practice and include up to date and innovative studies that cover issues which impact banking systems globally.

More information about this series at
http://www.palgrave.com/gp/series/14678

Rym Ayadi

Banking Business Models

Definition, Analytical Framework and Financial Stability Assessment

palgrave
macmillan

Rym Ayadi
CASS Business School
City University of London
London, UK

ISSN 2523-336X ISSN 2523-3378 (electronic)
Palgrave Macmillan Studies in Banking and Financial Institutions
ISBN 978-3-030-02247-1 ISBN 978-3-030-02248-8 (eBook)
https://doi.org/10.1007/978-3-030-02248-8

Library of Congress Control Number: 2019934099

Cover illustration: zozzzzo, iStock / Getty Images Plus

This Palgrave Macmillan imprint is published by the registered company Springer Nature Switzerland AG
The registered company address is: Gewerbestrasse 11, 6330 Cham, Switzerland

The updated version of the book can be found at
https://doi.org/10.1007/978-3-030-02248-8_13

Preface

This book consolidates several years of research and provides readers with a novel and comprehensive analysis on business models in banking, essential to understand bank businesses pre- and post-financial crisis and how they evolve in the financial system. A new definition of a business model based on a n asset-liability approach is provided and tested using a clustering methodology applied to large datasets in banks of Europe (32 countries), US and Canada (and credit unions). The banks business models (labelled as "BBM") identified are comprehensive, stable, comparable, updated annually and can serve for financial stability assessment and regulatory and resolution purpose.

The BBM datasets contain the business models indicators for banks in Europe (32 countries), US and Canada. The datasets containing the BBM outputs generated from the estimations and other constructed indicators that serve for the financial stability assessment will be made available to allow researchers to use it and integrate it in their research and policy analysis. Moreover, this book offers a unique analytical framework using the BBM analysis, complementary to the size and ownership structure analysis to assess performance, risk, response to regulation, resolution and systemic risk in banking pre- and post-financial crisis.

This book also provides regulators, supervisors and market participants with a comprehensive analytical framework and analysis to better understand the nature of risk attached to each bank business model and its contribution to systemic risk throughout the economic cycle.

This book will also guide postgraduate students on banking and finance delving into this topic.

The BBM data and research will be available on an online platform (www.BBM research.com). It will make available the list of indicators and their coverage rates, the methodologies used, the BBM codes and computations per bank, country and year. The BBM will be generated annually and published to promote research on this topic.

London, UK Rym Ayadi

Acknowledgements

The author would like to thank all the researchers who, over the years, have been involved and contributed to the bank business models research in particular Emrah Arbak and Willem Pieter De Groen at the Centre for European Policy Studies, Walid Mathlouthi and Michel Keoula at the International Research Centre on Cooperative Finance at HEC Montreal, Valerio Pesic at the University La Sapienza di Roma, and all the research assistants who have assisted in the research. She would also like to thank Professors Giovanni Ferri and Barbara Casu for their comments on the research undertaken over the years and their suggestions for improvements and J.C. Garcia for the valuable discussions on the topic.

Contents

List of Figures

List of Tables

CHAPTER 1

Introduction

Prior, during and in the aftermath of the Great Financial Crisis (GFC), banking has been undergoing fundamental changes. Following the major fallouts of large banking groups—in particular those with excessively risky **business models**, combined with the trillions incurred in losses and a wave of taxpayers-funded **bailouts**—a wave of **re-regulation** was undertaken to restore eroded market confidence and to safeguard **financial stability**. This led to major restructuring and waves of deleveraging, consolidation and emergence of new forms of finance with fundamental implications for the future of the **financial intermediation**.

In this changing context of evolving **market structures** and **financial regulations**, the bank business models (BBM) analysis emerged as a policy tool to better understand the nature of risk attached to banks and the relative contribution to each identified business model to **systemic risk** throughout the **economic cycle**.

The *business models analysis* for regulatory purpose was first introduced by Ayadi et al. (2011) in an initial attempt to screen and identify the business models of 26 **European banking institutions** and to assess their performance between prior and during the GFC, between 2006 and 2009. The exercise permitted a precise understanding of the balance sheet structure of banks and applied a data-driven simple **clustering analysis** to identify the business models of a small number of banks for regulatory purpose. The identification method showed the existence of three bank business models and indicated that the **retail banking model** has fared better

R. Ayadi, *Banking Business Models*, Palgrave Macmillan Studies in Banking and Financial Institutions,
https://doi.org/10.1007/978-3-030-02248-8_1

through the crisis in terms of performance, compared to the other identified business models, namely **investment business model** and **wholesale business model**, which displayed very risky behaviour before and during the financial crisis years. Business models analysis also proved to be relevant in that it demonstrated the unsuitability of the one-size-fits-all **Basel regulatory requirements**. In a subsequent research work by the same authors, *Regulation of European Banks and Business Models: Towards a New Paradigm*, Ayadi et al. (2012) shed light on the limitations of the Basel **Tier 1 capital ratio** and, hence, the **Basel II risk-weights system** and not only recommended the inclusion of a legally binding **leverage ratio** to tackle these regulatory limitations but also confirmed that regulatory requirements (capital, liquidity and leverage) should be adapted to bank business models to ensure they are better aligned with the underlying risk profiles of the different business models of banks. The authors also suggested an **annual monitoring** exercise of bank business models to better understand their evolution within macro- and micro-economic contexts. To test the relevance of this approach, the first pilot exercise on monitoring the business models of 147 banks in Europe was released in December 2014 in Ayadi and De Groen (2014). For the first time, a diverse dataset of banks of differing sizes and ownership structures was analysed using an easy applicable clustering methodology to identify business models and a new analytical framework was used to assess business models that included performance, risk and response to regulation. The findings reinforced previous conclusions and prepared the ground for more generalisation with larger datasets and more countries. In January 2016, a more comprehensive monitoring exercise was launched (Ayadi et al. 2016), which extended the sample from 147 banks to 2542 banks in 32 European countries, covering more than 95% of total assets of the European Union plus European Free Trade Association (EFTA) countries from 2005 to 2014 and accounting for 13,040 bank-year observations. The European Bank Business Models Monitor attempted to address the diversity of **bank sizes** and **ownership structures** in European countries and, hence, identify the response function of each business model in a **crisis situation**. In 2017, the same exercise was extended to US (Ayadi et al. 2017) and Canada (published in this book) to test whether the **BBM analysis** concept and approach can be used in other countries. The BBM research team will continue updating the dataset and expanding the data collection to other regions in the world thanks to a novel and broad definition tested and adopted to define a business model in banks (and other similar institutions such as credit unions).

The datasets and annual BBM analysis will be open access for research purposes (www.BBM research.com).

This book reviews the reasons and the process, describes the datasets in Europe, US and Canada, and details the methodology, computations and analysis used to develop the BBM analysis framework. It explains the relevance of this new framework for **financial stability assessment** and **future of regulation** and resolution.

First, it provides an overview on the evolving role of banks in the **financial system**—with a focus on why banks changed their business model over the past decades and how the economics literature explained it. Second, it proposes a definition after reviewing the literature on business models and banking and describes the datasets collected in Europe, US and Canada and the methodology used to identify business models in banks (and in credit unions in US and Canada subject to data availability) based on the book author's past and ongoing research. Third, it explains how the business models analysis can be a tool for financial stability assessment and can serve as a pillar for the future of regulation and resolution. Fourth, it provides the BBM assessment including the links with ownership and organisational structure and size, the **migration of business models**, the **assessment of performance** and **risks**, and how different business models respond to the exiting one-size-fits-all **regulation and resolution** using comprehensive datasets of banks in Europe, US and Canada.

The book is organised into 12 chapters and 7 appendices. Following the introduction, Chap. 2 delves into the reasons why business models in banks evolved as they did prior and in the aftermath of the GFC and provides key explanations from the literature on banking from economics and policy perspectives. Chapter 3 provides a novel definition of business models in banks after reviewing the literature on business models and banking and explaining the business model concept relevance to better understand what banks do. Chapter 4 describes the datasets of banks in Europe, US and Canada (and credit unions when data is available) studied and the methodology employed to identify business models in banks (and credit unions). Chapter 5 describes how business models in banks can be used in financial stability assessment. Chapters 6, 7, 8, 9, 10, and 11 offer the analysis on the interaction between business models, ownership, organisational structures and size, the analysis of migration of bank business models, the assessment of performance and risk and the response per bank business model to regulation and resolution. Finally, Chap. 12 concludes.

Most of the appendices provide supporting technical information about the banks surveyed and the methodology used.

References

Ayadi, R., E. Arbak and W.P. de Groen (2011), *Business Models in European Banking: A pre-and post-crisis screening*, Centre for European Policy Studies (CEPS), Brussels.

Ayadi, R., E. Arbak and W.P. de Groen (2012), *Regulation of European Banks and Business Models: Towards a new paradigm?*, Centre for European Policy Studies (CEPS), Brussels.

Ayadi, R. and W.P. de Groen (2014), "Banking Business Models Monitor 2014: Europe", Montreal, Joint Centre for European Policy Studies (CEPS) and International Observatory on Financial Service Cooperatives (IOFSC) publication (http://www.ceps.eu/book/banking-business-modelsmonitor-2014-europe).

Ayadi, R. et al. (2016), "Banking Business Models Monitor 2015: Europe", Montreal, International Research Centre On Cooperative Finance, HEC Montreal.

Ayadi, R. et al. (2017), "Bank and Credit Unions Business Models in the United States", Montreal, International Research Centre On Cooperative Finance, HEC Montreal.

CHAPTER 2

Changing Role of Banks in the Financial System

Several decades prior to the **Great Financial Crisis** (GFC), the structural features of banking and finance evolved, producing major changes on how banks and other financial institutions operate in the **financial system** domestically and worldwide. The traditional role of banks in the economy evolved from the **traditional intermediation approach** to a **one-stop shop**, in which banks offer a wide range of financial services, enhanced by a widespread wave of **financial innovations**. Banks and financial markets became more closely linked and integrated, which led to increasing systemic risk. More recently, **financial technology** (so-called Fintech) has created further disruptive forces and new risks in the financial industry that are yet to be explored in the upcoming decades.

This chapter exposes the evolving traditional role of banks which embraced the "**financialisation**" trend that led to a fundamental transformation of their original business model, and second it provides a literature review on the explanatory factors of this process of financial transformation, in particular the reasons why banks chose to diversify their activities and **funding strategies**.

R. Ayadi, *Banking Business Models*, Palgrave Macmillan Studies in Banking and Financial Institutions,
https://doi.org/10.1007/978-3-030-02248-8_2

2.1 Changing Role of Banks

Traditionally, banks have performed fundamental economic roles, mainly as liquidity providers, maturity transformers, risk managers and financial innovators. Depending on how properly they perform these roles during the macro-economic cycle, they either become shock absorbers or on the contrary shock originators.

Banks traditionally have information, risk analysis and monitoring advantages, which enable them to solve asymmetric information problems and hence mitigate *adverse selection* and *moral hazard*. Banks accept deposits and utilise their comparative advantages to transform deposits into loans. The bank accepts the credit (default) risk, holds the asset on its own balance sheet, monitors its borrowing customers and holds appropriate levels of capital to cover unexpected risk. It also effectively "insures" its loans internally through the risk premia incorporated into the rate of interest on loans. In this process, the bank offers an integrated service in that it performs all the core functions in the financial intermediation process.

Over the decades prior to the GFC, banks increased substantially their role of in the financial intermediation process. They become active players in the financial markets globally not only in the assets side via lending and investing short and long term but also on the liability side becoming more than ever active in the global interbank market and issuing short and long-term liability. They acted as insurance contracts sellers and buyers for risks of others and their own via the credit derivatives contracts. The rapid growth and overall size of banks in the economy became visible domestically, regionally and even globally. Beyond size, the leverage and interconnectedness of banks increased which led to blurring the traditional role of banks. This is coupled with the frenetic pace of financial innovation, some of which were used to optimise the minimum capital ratios required for the soundness of the banking sector. More recently, banks and other financial institutions are racing to benefit from the impressive financial technology wave that is already disrupting the traditional business models of banks.

In 2011, Ayadi et al. (2011) provided salient features of the process of increasing role and dominance of finance over the economy, a process known as "financialisation", which was due to several factors leading up to the GFC.

Ten years after the GFC these characteristics are only reinforced.

On the one hand, banks became and continue to be large players in the financial markets encouraged by the following interaction between demand and supply factors:

1. For many years, the macro-economic (i.e. a monetary policy that managed relatively low inflation leading up to a low interest rate environment) and regulatory (i.e. light-touch banking regulation environment) and the collective euphoria towards the frenetic race to returns of the pre-crisis years led to increase both the demand for loans and other financial products and the willingness of banks to meet that demand to maintain an upward cycle.
2. In the absence of a globally agreed leverage regulation till today, banks drove leverage to its highest levels and ensured that the capital consumption was minimised. The excess leverage and under-capitalisation led (and continue to lead) banks to expand faster and taking higher mispriced risk that is not backed by adequate levels of capital. This has increased the supply of loans and financial products that under-price the risk.
3. Banks reached high levels of profitability, which coupled with low cost of capital created further incentives for banks to continue driving the wave towards higher profitability with a fundamental mispricing of risks.[1] This process has provided incentives to all banks and non-banks active in the financial markets to further develop and grow to capture profits.

On the other hand, the increasing role of the interbank market has increased the exposures of banks to each others. Adding to this, the globalised nature of banking and finance and financial openness largely facilitated the free movement of capital and propagation of crises when they occur. When the macro-economic conditions were favourable, liquidity was abundant, which creates the false perception that liquidity is indefinite. On the opposite, when the macro-economic conditions deteriorate, then the liquidity evaporates and the confidence erodes.

[1] Due to the nature of the competitive environment at the time, banks adopted more short-term strategies to maximise the rate of return on equity. In turn, profitability was enhanced not by superior banking performance, but by banks raising their risk threshold and moving up the risk ladder without backing it by adequate level of capital. Internal reward and bonus structures created a bias towards short-termism and also towards excess risk-taking (Llewellyn 2010).

Each of these factors, both individually but especially in combination, created sufficient conditions for an overexpansion of banking activity and an artificially enhanced role of banks and other non-regulated financial institutions in the intermediation process in the upward trend of the macro-economic cycle.

Additionally, there were *fundamental structural factors* that aided the process of transformation and hence to these developments:

1. Since the early 1990s was the sharp rise in the pace of financial innovation, and especially in the use of credit derivatives designed to shift credit risk away from loan originators. This shift reduced the incentives of banks to screen and monitor their borrowers, which once were their raison d'être. The original incentives of banks have been altered. In the past, banks originate, underwrite risk and they manage it till maturity. With credit derivatives and particularly credit derivative swaps,[2] banks had little incentives to monitor the risks they underwrote till maturity.
2. The nature of bank risks also changed. **Securitisation** and other credit derivatives were designed specifically to shift credit risk and, for some years, they did just that. However, they also changed the nature of risk and, in particular, transformed credit risk into liquidity risk (buyers of the securities issued to purchase securitised assets from banks being unable to trade them), then into a funding risk (the securitising banks being unable to either sell assets at other than fire-sale prices or roll-over maturing debt), and ultimately into a solvency risk. The latter arose because banks were unable to sell assets in order to continue funding their securitisation programmes.
3. In the pre-crisis period, there was a massive rise in the volume of trading in complex, and sometimes opaque, derivatives contracts, coupled with the emergence of major trading platforms that made possible massive trading volumes.[3] Banks became exposed to capital markets and securities trading risks that they did not themselves manage or sometimes truly understand. In addition, over time, banks' holdings of liquid assets fell and their reliance on wholesale markets for liquidity and funding requirements increased.

[2] See Ayadi and Behr (2009).

[3] The Bank for International Settlements (BIS) has estimated that the notional amounts outstanding of over-the-counter (OTC) derivatives contracts to be USD 595 trillion at end of June 2018, an overall equivalent amount of USD 596 trillion at end of June 2007 before the fallout of Lehman.

4. Another equally important feature that emerges from the previous one is the more market-centric structure of financial systems, which implied a rise in the role of financial markets relative to institutions in the **financial intermediation process**. Furthermore, banks and markets became increasingly integrated (Boot and Thakor 2009). One of the many implications of this trend was that losses incurred in markets were at times translated into funding problems for banks. Furthermore, financial systems became more susceptible to market shocks, particularly in a continuous increase in **interconnectedness** and **network externalities**.[4]
5. The network externalities and the increasing connectedness of financial institutions with each other and with markets increased sharply in the years prior to the GFC. In the process, banks became exposed to capital market risks that they did not themselves manage or, in some cases, even understand. This increased connectedness meant that the number of banks that became potentially "systemically significant" increased. The increased connectedness arose through many channels, including, inter alia increased exposures in the interbank market, banks buying credit risk-shifting instruments and other derivatives issued by other banks, all banks trading in the same instruments and the reduced systemic diversity as banks adopted similar business models.

[4] Haldane (2009) defines the network as being both *complex* and *adaptive*: complex by virtue of the many interconnections within the network, and adaptive in that behaviour is driven by the interactions between optimising agents. He describes trends in the network as increased connectivity, there being a small number of hubs with multiple spokes, and the average path length within the network became shorter over time, leading to a small number of degrees of separation between countries and institutions. As a result, comparatively small shocks can have large systemic implications. Several factors contributed to the rise in network externalities, including the enhanced trading in derivatives (and credit derivatives in particular), the growing links between instruments and institutions, the increased globalisation of finance, the trend towards deregulation, banks diversifying into a wider range of business lines and into securities trading in particular, the growing homogeneity of banks in their business models, and the greater use by banks of wholesale market funding. Each of these trends had the effect of increasing the degree of connectedness between institutions and, as a result, the potential power of network externalities. Increased connectivity also complicated the monitoring of indirect counterparty risks. While bank A may be able to monitor its individual exposure to bank B, it becomes increasingly complex when bank B has a multitude of exposures within the network via derivatives and contingent liabilities, as this gives rise to indirect counterparty risks originating elsewhere in the network.

To complete the picture, largely unregulated "shadow banks", such as hedge funds and structured investment vehicles (SIVs) emerged as major new players in the financial intermediation process (Tett 2008) with all the risks and new sources of instabilities they bring.

As a consequence, banks developed new business models and moved away from their traditional model of **"originate-to-hold"** and "screen and monitor", whereby banks issue loans and hold the risk in their books. The emergence of new business models focused largely, though not entirely, on new credit risk-shifting instruments and market activities on the assets, liability and off-balance sheet.

In the years leading up to the crisis, the balance sheet structure of banks transformed and several trends in bank business models emerged:

- Banks increasingly diversified into more lines of business activity, some of which had previously been prohibited by regulation, such as trading and propriety trading.
- Securitisation of loans became a central business strategy for many banks and this securitisation was transferred in conduits with no public information on them.
- Investment and trading activity increased sharply, and the proportion of traded assets in the total balance sheet rose substantially in many cases.
- Banks reduced their holdings of liquid assets as they developed greater access to wholesale funding markets, which made their debt liability riskier to match with equally risky assets.
- The extent of maturity transformation also increased sharply as greater use was made of short-maturity money market funding sources.
- An increased dependency developed on wholesale and money market funding, which increased the dependency on interest rates policies.

These business alterations to the traditional model of the banking firm meant that banks were no longer required to perform all the functions in the bank intermediation process. Banks stopped behaving in the traditional way as market-makers in credit risk and, in effect, came to act as brokers in credit risk between ultimate borrowers and those who either purchased asset-backed securities or who offered credit derivative insurance. Beyond the balance sheets of banks, which become ever more diversified towards market activities, the off-balance sheet became ever more important and relying on the balance sheet only do not longer provide the real picture of banks' activities.

2.2 Literature on the Changing Role of Banks

The literature provides several reasons why banks may choose to diversify their business models instead of specialising in a narrow range of activities.

This was the building block of the diversification argument summarised in Ayadi et al. (2011) in their first research attempt to screen the business models of banks in Europe. First, the informational advantage: by providing a service, banks gain valuable information on their clients that might provide advantages in the provision of other services (Sharpe 1990; Diamond 1991; Rajan 1992). Second, the diversification benefit and reduction in risks: by engaging in a wide range of activities, banks may also reduce their risks through diversification and economies of scope (Diamond 1984). Lastly, the competitive struggle: as **regulatory reforms** diminish competitive inequalities, banks with different models compete with one another, providing incentives to offer a broader range of products to their customers. Many banks have also adjusted their business profiles to reflect changes in the demographic structure of their retail client base.

Additionally, in Europe the 1999 **Financial Services Action Plan** (FSAP) provided a minimally harmonised regulatory environment for banks and other financial institutions to operate. This has created a new competitive environment for banks to become one-stop shop institutions that offer all types of financial services with no restrictions.

Although **diversification** may prove beneficial to the bank, it may also endanger social welfare. A typical bank-client relationship can harbour a variety of conflicts of interests, providing **informational advantages** to banks vis-à-vis the market. For example, first-hand information on borrowers may enable a bank to extract monopolistic rents to "lock-in" the customer to its services in the future (Sharpe 1990; Rajan 1992). These incumbent advantages may hinder competition in the market by acting as barriers to entry (Dell'Ariccia et al. 1999; Marquez 2002). Alternatively, confronted with exclusive information about the financial health of their clients, banks may underwrite a troubled firm's securities despite known risks, in an attempt to secure the repayment of earlier loans (Kanatas and Qi 1998).

The potential for conflicts of interests underlines the modern versions of the arguments raised against the "universal banks" in the aftermath of the Great Depression. The **US Glass-Steagall Act** of 1933 imposed such a separation or a "firewall" between the securities and commercial (retail) activities of banks. In the years that followed, some of the European countries also imposed similar restrictions to limit the emergence of universal banks. The repeal of the Glass-Steagall Act in 1999 and the initiatives in the EU in the 1980s and 1990s, most notably the Second Banking Directive (1989/646/EEC), have been the main drivers for the re-diversification of the banking models on both sides of the Atlantic.[5] As a result of these developments, the banks have turned increasingly to non-interest income sources and non-traditional activities. Moreover, the low interest rate environment also provides incentives to banks to diversify their income streams from intermediation activities.

Whilst diversification of individual banks might seem to reduce their overall risk and may be one of the central motives, there is also a systemic dimension to consider as this might make the system as a whole less diversified. Andy Haldane (2009) of the Bank of England suggests that as banks diversified into each others' traditional areas, and most especially into the capital markets business, the system became less diverse and, therefore, potentially more vulnerable to common shocks. Furthermore, the diversification of banks into derivatives trading also has a systemic dimension. Many commentators (and central bankers) argued before the crisis that credit-risk-shifting derivatives should make the system less risky because risks were spread more optimally. However, this seems not to have been the experience during the crisis. Rajan (1992) has suggested that these new instruments might have made the system less vulnerable in the face of small, uncorrelated shocks, but more vulnerable to large, correlated shocks.

The recent deregulation drive was supported by arguments to allow banks to achieve more favourable economies of scope and better diversification of

[5] The diversified banking model reappeared in Europe prior to the Second Banking Directive of 1989. The Directive and the accompanying regulations have only harmonised the legal and regulatory framework applicable to all types of banks. In an attempt to enhance integration within the EU's internal market, the single banking passport was introduced, facilitating cross-border businesses and introducing common regulatory and supervisory standards. The regulations have nevertheless enhanced the expansion opportunities of EU banks, both geographically and in scope.

risks (Barth et al. 2000).[6] The arguments were largely backed by evidence that failed to show substantial differences in the quality of securities underwritten by the universal banks and specialised investment houses (Kroszner and Rajan 1994; Puri 1994).

How does the **universal banking model** fare in terms of risk-taking, performance and efficiency in the light of recent evidence? A number of empirical studies have addressed this question. The common finding is that although diversification may expand the range of opportunities, these benefits may be more than offset by the costs from increased exposure to volatility (DeYoung and Roland 2001; Stiroh 2004, 2006; Stiroh and Rumble 2006). Focarelli et al. (2011) show that securities underwritten by universal banks are riskier than those underwritten by specialised investment houses. The authors, however, argue that the increased risk-taking is due to an attempt to expand market share, and not conflicts of interest. Others have found that although diversification may enhance market valuations, expanding banks hold much less capital and engage in more risky activities (Demsetz and Strahan 1997; Baele et al. 2007; Demirgüç-Kunt and Huizinga 2010b).

An important development in the banking sectors in most developing countries since the 1990s is the rapid growth of securitisation and structured products.[7] In a nutshell, **securitisation** allows banks to pool their risky assets and sell them to outside investors, potentially transferring the associated credit risks to the markets.[8] Traditionally, the growth in these transactions has been justified by the mutual benefits they offer to both investors and originators. From the point of view of the investors, buying the products has been attractive due to the diversification benefits—as long as the products are not correlated with other holdings. From the

[6] The discussion on the separation of banks' activities resurfaced in the midst of the financial crisis in the US during the deliberations for the Dodd-Frank Wall Street Reform and Consumer Protection Act. The original proposal, endorsed by President Obama in January 2010, contained the so-called Volcker rule which would have prohibited banks from engaging in purely proprietary trading and put severe restrictions on owning or investing in hedge funds or private equity funds. A much watered-down version of the bill was enacted in June 2010, which allowed banks to engage in a broader range of proprietary trading activities.

[7] As argued in Duffee and Zhou (2001), among other structured products, credit default swaps can also be used for the purpose of transferring risks to other investors.

[8] See Neal (1996) for an early discussion on the use of structured products for controlling credit risk. See also Brunnermeier (2009, pp. 78–82) for a concise description of securitisation and other structured products.

lender's perspective, the transaction eliminates exposure to risks and, in the case of regulated entities, reduces required capital charges.

The benign view of securitisation and structured products has been challenged during the 2007–2009 financial crisis. To summarise, the rising popularity of these transactions has led to a "flood of cheap credit" and growth of an interconnected institutions that are not regulated, or **"shadow banks"** (Brunnermeier 2009; Pozsar et al. 2010). A particularly critical argument has been the effect of securitisation on credit standards. Since most credit risks are borne by outside investors, banks had little incentive to properly screen (and monitor) loans.[9] There is mounting empirical evidence that credit standards were indeed incrementally lowered in the US prior to the crisis (Mian and Sufi 2009; Keys et al. 2010). There are also questions concerning the extent to which the originators were able to offload their risks. Although the special purpose vehicles (SPVs) are, at least in theory, legally separate entities, the originating institution nevertheless had substantial exposures from the liquidity enhancements and forms of retained interests (Gorton et al. 2006). Indeed, originating institutions have taken a substantial part of the losses during the crisis, achieving "securitisation without risk transfer" (Greenlaw et al. 2008; Shin 2009; Acharya et al. 2010a). According to these arguments, structured products are attractive because they allowed the originating institutions to expand their balance sheets while reducing their capital charges, potentially facilitating regulatory arbitrage.[10]

A parallel development to the diversification of banking activities has been the diversification of funding strategies.

Over the past few years, many banks have reduced their reliance on traditional retail depositors and turned to short-term funding in the interbank and wholesale markets. In essence, short-term funds allow banks to manage their balance sheet sizes actively in a highly pro-cyclical manner (Adrian and Shin 2008, 2010). In this manner, the diversification of funding strategies is an offshoot of the increasing trading activities. For banks

[9] The concern that securitisation may lower credit standards is not new. Gorton and Pennacchi (1995) model a bank's choice between holding loans and selling them, focusing on the potential for moral hazard. They conclude that if the banks hold a certain fraction of the securitised loans (or provide limited recourse), then the moral hazard problem could be partly mitigated. See also Ayadi and Behr (2009) for a similar argument for the credit derivatives markets.

[10] See also Jones (2000) on the potential use of structured products and derivative transactions for achieving regulatory arbitrage.

that engage heavily in trading, when the value of mark-to-market securities increases, their equity also increases. The institutions use this "surplus capacity" to expand their balance sheets even further by borrowing and issuing new securities. Repurchase agreements (repos) and reverse repurchase agreements (reverse repos), in which a financial institution sells a security (or buys it, in the case a reverse repo) to buy (or sell) it back later, are extremely suitable for this purpose. Institutions may also expand their activities and borrowing through the use of **off-balance sheet special purpose vehicles** (Acharya et al. 2010b).

The literature provides divergent views on the impact of the increased use of these short-term funding (and lending) alternatives. The "bright-side" argument suggests that relying more on market funding may enhance market discipline. Provided that they are credibly excluded from the safety net, holders of subordinated debt may perform monitoring roles that cannot be fulfilled by the small and dispersed depositor holders (Calomiris and Kahn 1991; Calomiris 1999). More pessimistically, however, the market's monitoring incentives could be undermined by the expectation of government intervention in the "**too big to fail**" (TBTF) banks, that is, **moral hazard**. When a bailout is a credible likelihood, the market's perception of risk may diverge substantially from the stand-alone risk represented by the bank's operations. Apart from weakening the debt-holders' incentives to apply monitoring and market discipline, that is, moral hazard, such imperfections may also motivate banks to become large enough to be considered too big to fail.[11] There is some empirical evidence (also supported by this study) suggesting that banks that are judged to be TBTF receive a superior rating, other things being equal, which in turn lowers the cost of market funding.

Another argument against the heavy use of short-term funding is the potential drying-up of liquidity in the event of a crisis. When banks become reliant on short-term financing, such as overnight repos, they need to roll over a substantial part of their funding on a daily basis, making them severely exposed to a sudden drying-up of liquidity. **Short-term lending**, such as reverse-repo transactions, also exposes institutions to liquidity risk, seriously undermining the value of any collateral backing the transaction. In short, the trend towards the increasing use of these short-term

[11] Banks may also outgrow their optimal size and may overextend their activities if doing so allows the management to extract private benefits, such as more power or compensation or to build empires (Jensen and Meckling 1976; Jensen 1986).

instruments was seen to be among the chief explanations for the cataclysmic setbacks faced by some banks in the early phases of the financial crisis (Brunnermeier 2009; Adrian and Shin 2010).

By and large, the literature has confirmed that state support is likely to dampen the risks of debt-holders (even if the bank is inherently risky), potentially giving rise to increased moral hazard. O'Hara and Shaw (1990) find evidence of net positive wealth effects accruing to large US banks covered by the partial **deposit insurance** schemes put in place in the mid-1980s. Kane (2000) and Benston et al. (1995) show that bank mergers and acquisitions in the same period were partly motivated by the aim of creating institutions that were large enough to be covered by the US deposit insurance system. In addition to the gains for shareholders, Penas and Unal (2004) find that bond-holders also stand to benefit from state support that is granted to too-big-to-fail institutions. Implicit government insurance effectively serves to weaken (if not reverse) the correlation between individual bank risk and debenture yields (Flannery and Sorescu 1996). Moreover, the sensitivity of the subordinated note spreads to measures of stand-alone risk is lower for state-owned banks and during periods of fiscal ease, that is, when government support is more credible (Sironi 2003).[12]

The empirical literature has therefore provided ample support to the idea that the monitoring roles of debt-holders may be undermined when state intervention is judged to be likely. Moreover, owing to their ability to pull back from the markets relatively quickly, short-term creditors may also have fewer incentives to conduct proper monitoring (Huang and Ratnovski 2010). This would offset one of the key arguments for supporting the diversification of the funding strategies. As the recent financial crisis amply demonstrated, an excessive reliance on market funding may also invite other risks, such as a sudden drying-up of liquidity. Even small changes in an institution's underlying value can lead to a "catastrophic drop" in roll-over debt capacity and deleveraging, much like the one that was observed in the early phases of the crisis (Acharya et al. 2010b; Acharya and Viswanathan 2011). Recent evidence supports these arguments, showing that non-deposit wholesale funding increases bank fragility (Demirgüç-Kunt and Huizinga 2010b).

[12] In a similar vein, Demirgüç-Kunt and Huizinga (2010a) provide evidence that during the 2007–2009 financial crisis, large banks saw a deterioration of their market valuations and credit default swap spreads in countries with large public deficits.

To sum up, the economics literature has provided a number of reasons why banks seek to diversify their activities and funding strategies and hence to redefine their business model—if a business model can be represented as the interaction between the initial activities and funding strategies of banks. However, diversification may in some cases undermine social welfare and **financial stability**, especially in the presence of informational rents, conflicts of interest and moral hazard risks. In view of the GFC, the recent literature singles out the excessive reliance on market-based or **wholesale funding** as a potentially harmful practice. These concerns are particularly acute when market participants have little incentive to monitor the banks due to the **implicit or explicit government guarantees** enjoyed by the banks and their creditors.

References

Ayadi, R., E. Arbak and W.P. de Groen (2011), *Business Models in European Banking: A pre-and post-crisis screening*, Centre for European Policy Studies (CEPS), Brussels.

Acharya, V.V., P. Schnabl and G. Suarez (2010a), "Securitization without risk transfer", NBER Working Papers, No. 15730, National Bureau of Economic Research, Cambridge, MA.

Acharya, V.V., D. Gale and T. Yorulmazer (2010b), "Rollover Risk and Market Freezes", NBER Working Papers, No. 15674, National Bureau of Economic Research, Cambridge, MA.

Acharya, V.V. and S. Viswanathan (2011), "Leverage, Moral Hazard, and Liquidity", *Journal of Finance*, Vol. 66, No. 1, pp. 99–138.

Adrian, T. and H.S. Shin (2008), "Financial Intermediary Leverage and Value-at-Risk", Federal Reserve Bank of New York Staff Reports, No. 338, Federal Reserve Bank of New York, New York, NY.

Adrian, T. and H.S. Shin (2010), "Liquidity and Leverage", *Journal of Financial Intermediation*, Vol. 19, No. 3, pp. 418–437.

Ayadi, R. and P. Behr (2009), "On the Necessity to Regulate Credit Derivatives Markets", *Journal of Banking Regulation*, Vol. 10, No. 3, pp. 179–201.

Baele, L., O. De Jonghe and R. Vander Vennet (2007), "Does the Stock Market Value Bank Diversification?", *Journal of Banking and Finance*, Vol. 31, No. 7, pp. 1999–2023.

Barth, J.R., R.D. Brumbaugh Jr. and J.A. Wilcox (2000), "The Repeal of Glass-Steagall and the Advent of Broad Banking", OCC Economic Working Paper, No. 2000-5, US Office of the Comptroller of the Currency, Washington, DC, April.

Benston, G.J., W.C. Hunter and L.D. Wall (1995), "Motivations for Bank Mergers and Acquisitions: Enhancing the Deposit Insurance Put Option versus Earnings Diversification", *Journal of Money, Credit, and Banking*, Vol. 27, No. 3, pp. 777–788.

Boot, A.W. and A.V. Thakor (2009), "The Accelerating Integration of Banks and Markets and its Implications for Regulation", in A. Berger, P. Molyneux and J. Wilson (eds), *The Oxford Handbook of Banking*, Oxford: Oxford University Press.

Brunnermeier, M.K. (2009), "Symposium: Early Stages of the Credit Crunch: Deciphering the Liquidity and Credit Crunch 2007–2008", *Journal of Economic Perspectives*, Winter, Vol. 23, No. 1, pp. 77–100.

Calomiris, C.W. (1999), "Building an Incentive-Compatible Safety Net", *Journal of Banking and Finance*, Vol. 23, No. 10, pp. 1499–1519.

Calomiris, C.W. and C.M. Kahn (1991), "The Role of Demandable Debt in Structuring Optimal Banking Arrangements", *American Economic Review*, Vol. 81, No. 3, pp. 497–513.

Dell'Ariccia, G., E. Friedman and R. Marquez (1999), "Adverse Selection as a Barrier to Entry in the Banking Industry", *RAND Journal of Economics*, Autumn, Vol. 30, No. 3, pp. 515–534.

Demirgüç-Kunt, A. and H. Huizinga (2010a), "Are banks too big to fail or too big to save? International evidence from equity prices and CDS spreads", World Bank Policy Research Working Paper Series, No. 5360, World Bank, Washington, DC.

Demirgüç-Kunt, A. and H. Huizinga (2010b), "Bank Activity and Funding Strategies: The Impact on Risk and Returns", *Journal of Financial Economics*, Vol. 98, No. 3, pp. 626–650.

Demsetz, R.S. and P.E. Strahan (1997), "Diversification, Size, and Risk at Bank Holding Companies", *Journal of Money, Credit and Banking*, Vol. 29, No. 3, pp. 300–313.

DeYoung, R. and K.P. Roland (2001), "Product Mix and Earnings Volatility at Commercial Banks: Evidence from a Degree of Total Leverage Model", *Journal of Financial Intermediation*, Vol. 10, No. 1, pp. 54–84.

Diamond, D.W. (1984), "Financial Intermediation and Delegated Monitoring", *Review of Economic Studies*, Vol. 51, No. 3, pp. 393–414.

Diamond, D.W. (1991), "Monitoring and Reputation: The Choice between Bank Loans and Directly Placed Debt", *Journal of Political Economy*, Vol. 99, No. 4, pp. 689–721.

Duffee, G.R. and C. Zhou (2001), "Credit Derivatives in Banking: Useful Tools for Managing Risk?", *Journal of Monetary Economics*, Vol. 48, No. 1, pp. 25–54.

Flannery, M.J. and S.M. Sorescu (1996), "Evidence of Bank Market Discipline in Subordinated Debenture Yields: 1983–1991", *Journal of Finance*, Vol. 51, No. 4, pp. 1347–1377.

Focarelli, D., D. Marques-Ibanez and A.F. Pozzolo (2011), "Are universal banks better underwriters? Evidence from the last days of the Glass-Steagall Act", ECB Working Paper Series, No. 1287, European Central Bank, Frankfurt.

Gorton, G.B. and G.G. Pennacchi (1995), "Banks and Loan Sales: Marketing Nonmarketable Assets", *Journal of Monetary Economics*, Vol. 35, No. 3, pp. 389–411.

Gorton, G.B., N.S. Souleles, M. Carey and R.M. Stulz (2006), "Special Purpose Vehicles and Securitization", in *The Risks of Financial Institutions*, A National Bureau of Economic Research Conference Report, Chicago and London: University of Chicago Press, pp. 549–597.

Greenlaw, D., J. Hatzius, A.K. Kashyap and H.S. Shin (2008), "Leveraged Losses: Lessons from the Mortgage Market Meltdown", US Monetary Policy Forum Report, No. 2, Rosenberg Institute, Brandeis International Business School and Initiative on Global Markets, University of Chicago Graduate School of Business.

Haldane, A. (2009), "Rethinking the Financial Network", speech to Financial Student Association, Amsterdam, April (http://www.bankofengland.co.uk/publications/speeches/2009/speech409.pdf).

Huang, R. and L. Ratnovski (2010), "The Dark Side of Bank Wholesale Funding", IMF Working Papers, No. 10/170, International Monetary Fund, Washington, DC.

Jensen, M.C. (1986), "Agency Costs of Free Cash Flow, Corporate Finance, and Takeovers", *American Economic Review*, Vol. 76, No. 2, pp. 323–329.

Jensen, M.C. and W.H. Meckling (1976), "Theory of the Firm: Managerial Behavior, Agency Costs and Ownership Structure", *Journal of Financial Economics*, Vol. 3, No. 4, pp. 305–360.

Jones, D. (2000), "Emerging Problems with the Basel Capital Accord: Regulatory Capital Arbitrage and Related Issues", *Journal of Banking and Finance*, Vol. 24, Nos. 1–2, pp. 35–58.

Kanatas, G. and J. Qi (1998), "Underwriting by Commercial Banks: Incentive Conflicts, Scope Economies, and Project Quality", *Journal of Money, Credit, and Banking*, Vol. 30, No. 1, pp. 119–133.

Kane, E.J. (2000), "Incentives for Banking Megamergers: What Motives Might Regulators Infer from Event-Study Evidence?", *Journal of Money, Credit, and Banking*, Vol. 32, No. 3, pp. 671–701.

Keys, B.J., T. Mukherjee, A. Seru and V. Vig (2010), "Did Securitization Lead to Lax Screening? Evidence from Subprime Loans", *Quarterly Journal of Economics*, Vol. 125, No. 1, pp. 307–362.

Kroszner, R.S. and R.G. Rajan (1994), "Is the Glass-Steagall Act Justified? A Study of the U.S. Experience with Universal Banking before 1933", *American Economic Review*, Vol. 84, No. 4, pp. 810–832.

Llewellyn, D.T (2010), "*The Global Banking Crisis and the Post-Crisis Banking and Regulatory Scenario*", Research Papers in Corporate Finance, University of Amsterdam.

Marquez, R. (2002), "Competition, Adverse Selection, and Information Dispersion in the Banking Industry", *Review of Financial Studies*, Summer, Vol. 15, No. 3, pp. 901–926.

Mian, A. and A. Sufi (2009), "The Consequences of Mortgage Credit Expansion: Evidence from the U.S. Mortgage Default Crisis", *Quarterly Journal of Economics*, Vol. 124, No. 4, pp. 1449–1496.

Neal, R.S. (1996), "Credit Derivatives: New Financial Instruments for Controlling Credit Risk", *Federal Reserve Bank of Kansas City Economic Review*, 2nd Quarter, Vol. 81, No. 2, pp. 14–27.

O'Hara, M. and W. Shaw (1990), "Deposit Insurance and Wealth Effects: The Value of Being 'Too Big to Fail'", *Journal of Finance*, Vol. 45, No. 5, pp. 1587–1600.

Penas, M.F. and H. Unal (2004), "Gains in Bank Mergers: Evidence from the Bond Markets", *Journal of Financial Economics*, Vol. 74, No. 1, pp. 149–179.

Pozsar, Z., T. Adrian, A. Ashcraft and H. Boesky (2010), "Shadow Banking", Staff Reports, No. 458, Federal Reserve Bank of New York Staff Reports, New York, NY, July.

Puri, M. (1994), "The Long-Term Default Performance of Bank Underwritten Security Issues", *Journal of Banking and Finance*, Vol. 18, No. 2, pp. 397–418.

Rajan, R.G. (1992), "Insiders and Outsiders: The Choice between Informed and Arm's-Length Debt", *Journal of Finance*, Vol. 47, No. 4, pp. 1367–1400.

Sharpe, S.A. (1990), "Asymmetric Information, Bank Lending, and Implicit Contracts: A Stylized Model of Customer Relationships", *Journal of Finance*, Vol. 45, No. 4, pp. 1069–1087.

Shin, H.S. (2009), "Securitisation and Financial Stability", *Economic Journal*, Vol. 119, No. 536, pp. 309–332.

Sironi, A. (2003), "Testing for Market Discipline in the European Banking Industry: Evidence from Subordinated Debt Issues", *Journal of Money, Credit, and Banking*, Vol. 35, No. 3, pp. 443–472.

Stiroh, K.J. (2004), "Diversification in Banking: Is Non-interest Income the Answer?", *Journal of Money, Credit, and Banking*, Vol. 36, No. 5, pp. 853–882.

Stiroh, K.J. (2006), "A Portfolio View of Banking with Interest and Non-interest Activities", *Journal of Money, Credit, and Banking*, Vol. 38, No. 5, pp. 1351–1361.

Stiroh, K.J. and A. Rumble (2006), "The Dark Side of Diversification: The Case of US Financial Holding Companies", *Journal of Banking and Finance*, Vol. 30, No. 8, pp. 2131–2161.

Tett, G. (2008), "Leaders at wits' end as markets throw one tantrum after another", *Financial Times*, 11 October.

CHAPTER 3

Defining a Business Model in Banks

The business model is multi-faceted and complex concept. It is a relatively new concept and is ill defined in banks but is widely used by scholars and policy analysts when assessing these institutions.

This chapter attempts to define what a **business model** is in banks.

First, it provides a brief overview on the business model concept and a bank in the literature. Second, it exposes the definition proposed by the author of what a business model is in banks and other similar institutions.

3.1 What Is a Business Model?

Although the growth in popularity for the subject has translated into several scientific contributions that try to develop and clarify the concept of a business model (Achtenhagen et al. 2013), the variety of the fields in which it is used compromises the emergence of a unified concept that is widely accepted.

The business model concept has been extensively examined in the management and business literature, much less in economics and finance.

There are two main ways authors in the management/business and strategy fields address the definition of a business model: a component approach and a concept approach. The component approach gives the elements that can define a business model, whereas the concept approach

R. Ayadi, *Banking Business Models*, Palgrave Macmillan Studies in Banking and Financial Institutions,
https://doi.org/10.1007/978-3-030-02248-8_3

provides the information that should be given by a business model. Many authors combine both approaches in their contributions.

Commonly, a business model is defined as the plan implemented by a company to generate revenue and make a profit from operations. One of the early attempts to clarify the concept is found in Osterwalder et al. (2005). The authors propose the following definition: *a business model is a conceptual tool that contains a set of elements and their relationships and allows expressing the business logic of a specific firm. It is a description of the value a company offers to one or several segments of customers and of the architecture of the firm and its network of partners for creating, marketing and delivering this value and relationship capital, to generate profitable and sustainable revenue streams.*

In his study Teece (2010) explains that a business model is specific to a particular firm and defines a business model as "*the design or architecture of the value creation, delivery, and capture mechanisms*".

Osterwalder and Pigneur (2010) define a business model as "*the rationale of how an organization creates, delivers, and captures value*". According to the same authors, who focus on its evolution and its place in a firm, a business model can be described through nine building blocks that show how the organisation intends to make money: customer segments, value proposition, channels, customer relationships, revenue streams, key resources, key activities, key partnerships and cost structure.

The nine blocks cover four main areas of a business: customers, offer, infrastructure and financial viability.

Other authors feature the interrelations with technology and the virtues of an adaptation of the business model. Investigating the conditions under which a technology can be successfully adopted by a firm, Chesbrough (2010) puts an emphasis on the functions fulfilled by a business model to define the concept as an articulation of the following constituents: development of a value proposition, determination of the appropriate market segment and the revenue generation mechanism, estimation of costs structure, assessment of the position of the firm in the value chain, identification of complementors and competitors, and formulation of the competitive strategy. As well, the paper of Baden-Fuller and Haefliger (2013) emphasises the interplay between technological innovation and business model possibilities and Achtenhagen et al. (2013) point out that the business model should adapt over time in order for the firm to achieve sustained value creation.

The communality of these academic contributions is how an organisation achieves value creation while interacting with its consumers, suppliers and regulators (if the company is a regulated entity).

For the purpose of our analysis, bearing in mind the emerging common themes pointed out by Zott et al. (2011) in their extensive literature review can be the first step to attempt to tailor one or more of these themes to define a business model in financial organisations with a particular emphasis on banks:

1. The Business model is emerging as a new unit of analysis;
2. Business models emphasise a system-level, holistic approach to explaining how firms "do business";
3. Firms' activities play an important role in the various conceptualisations of Business Models that have been proposed; and
4. Business models seek to explain how value is created, not just how it is captured.

These themes are all pointing to the relevance to a business model as a unit of analysis, the importance to have a holistic approach to understand how a firm does business in the market(s) where it operates and the role of the activities to conceptualise the business model analysis while exploring the dynamics of value creation and destruction.

As the intention of this chapter in this book is to provide a working definition of a business model in banks, a definition of a bank as such is worth recalling.

3.2 What Is a Bank?

Before embarking in the definition aspects of what a bank is, it is useful to first recall the role of financial intermediaries in a market economy. Like other intermediaries, financial intermediaries buy and sell products and services of their industry: financial claims. They are firms that transform size, risk and maturity of financial claims (Gurley et al. 1960). Banks take, transform and manage risk.

Common justifications of their raison d'être put forth in the theory of industrial organisation in economics apply, namely frictions (costs and indivisibilities) and non-convexities in transaction technologies (Benston and Smith 1976) frequently associated with market failures. Freixas and Rochet (2008) make the point that transaction costs in financial intermediation are to be understood broadly, not only in terms of physical and technological costs but also in terms **of informational asymmetries** (**adverse selection**, **moral hazard** and costly state verification).

Clearly, economies of scale and economies of scope lower physical and technological transaction costs for financial intermediaries. More explicitly, financial intermediaries will act at the same time as coalition of depositors seeking to smooth their consumption across intertemporal contingencies (Diamond and Dybvig 1983), and coalition of borrowers pooling their risks, thus enabling them to lower the cost of capital (Leland and Pyle 1977).

Among financial intermediaries, a feature of banking firms is the collection of deposits (including demand deposits) of the public and the granting of loans. These are financial contracts, which in contrast to other financial claims are not easily transferrable (Freixas and Rochet 2008). In addition, the province of banks is the management of the payment system indispensable to economic activity. This unique role that translates into information gathering has created a competitive advantage for banks over the other financial intermediaries. In particular, they are in a better position to alter the informational asymmetries between savers and borrowers by a more efficient screening and monitoring of borrowers (Diamond 1984).

In addition, the fractional reserve system enables banks to grant loans or make investments and commitments that are large multiples of the deposits collected. This is a source of vulnerability since keeping confidence of depositors is paramount. To safeguard that essential role of savings collection, most governments in developed countries put into place a deposit insurance scheme to guarantee the reimbursement of modest amounts of deposit. The reassuring effect of the deposit insurance scheme is essential to avoid bank runs but there is evidence that the scheme has increased the risky behaviour of depository institutions (Cull et al. 2004). This is commonly known as moral hazard. These two schemes (fractional reserve system and deposit insurance) provide a rationale for a solvency regulation of the banking system, beyond free market and competition concerns.

Owing to the broad scope of policy concerns about the banking industry, economists have developed in the last few decades some analytical tools for the measurement of bank output and performance. Indeed, the determination of the optimal output mix, scale size and balance sheet management strategies are crucial from a regulatory perspective. Measuring the outputs and performance has been essential to define what a bank does and whether and how it performs from an industrial economic standpoint. However, this approach does not take into account the risk taken by banks and its evolution in the system.

Traditionally, in economic theory, two principle approaches have been used for the measurement of the output of a bank as an attempt to define banks: the production approach and the intermediation approach.

The production approach attempts to estimate cost functions and possible economies of scale, analyse their sources and implications for regulatory purposes (Benston 1965; Bell and Murphy 1968). This approach is dominated by a specification of a functional form for the production function and the use of physical units of inputs and outputs (number of deposits, number of loans and number of accounts).

The intermediation value approach is credited for a better micro-economic foundation (Freixas and Rochet 2008, p. 119). In the seminal paper of this stream of the literature, Sealey and Lindley (1977) contend that physical units of the output of a financial firm should be measured by the dollar value of earning assets, which should be the analogous of the physical units of a non-financial firm. The empirical study of Murray and White (1980) applies that approach to Credit Unions of British Columbia to derive some regulatory policy conclusions. More recent contributions (namely Ayadi et al. 2013) adopt the same approach to investigate efficiency gains in mergers and acquisitions in the banking industry and to consequently deliver some policy implications.

In these approaches, the bank is considered as a production function that either produces deposits or credits or transforming deposits to credits. However, this is a simplification of reality and as mentioned already does not take into account the risk taken by banks when credits are granted.

In closing this section, the current dominant paradigm of the neoclassical economic theory posits that the only social responsibility of a firm is profit maximisation and therefore the **shareholder-value approach** of the micro-economic theory of the firm. The financial crisis of 2007–2008 has brought about a renewal of interest in an alternative approach to the study of the economic behaviour of large corporations and banks that is: the **stakeholder-value approach** (Ayadi et al. 2009, 2010) that takes into account other interests beyond the shareholder's interests. Magill et al. (2015) is a recent attempt to build such a theory. Essentially, the stakeholder value is the result of the maximisation of the welfare of shareholders, workers and consumers. **Financial cooperatives** and **credit unions** qualify for stakeholder financial institutions. They collect deposit and provide credits among other activities, but they do not maximise the shareholders' value since they do not have shareholders. They have members and they strive to maximise the member surplus (Ayadi et al. 2010).

The business model approach applied to the banking industry with diverse **ownership structures** could offer an alternative to understand and assess how banks operate and whether and how they perform. Depending on the definition of the business model adopted, it can accommodate value creation but also value destruction in the dynamics of transformation.

3.3 A Business Model in Banks

Defining a business model of a financial institution in general and a bank in particular is not a trivial task. As was exposed previously, the economic literature traditionally defines a bank using the production or the intermediation approach. The growing level of diversification of banks in terms of activities and funding strategies over the years prior to the financial crisis has fundamentally changed the traditional view of how banks are defined and how they intermediate in the economy. Banks do not only collect deposits and grant credits but they became financial diversified houses that beyond traditional activities get market/wholesale funding and invest short to long term via equity, structured financial instruments and other more complex financial structures. Moreover, banks are key players in the financial system as institutions (small, medium or large) and also in the financial markets. Their role can be appreciated: (1) via their evolving balance sheets and off-balance sheets over the years and how they interact in the financial system in general and financial markets in particular; and (2) how they contribute to risk accumulation in the system—in other words how and at which speed they contribute to systemic risk.

A bank definition that only provides a partial view of what a bank does tends to mask the activities that form a major part of what banks do and how they contribute to systemic risk.

To assess business models, economists use income breakdown (i.e. traditional intermediation activities vs others financial markets activities) indicators to define a business model of banks. Using the income generated from banking activities in general is an explicit recognition that a bank captures and creates value (i.e. assessed by the financial income generated). However, it does not recognise that this income may have also generated an excessive amount of risk in the system that is not captured in the production and/or revenue function of a bank.

The business model concept has been a popular concept among management scholars and was used to understand how firms operate and create value in an overall dynamic of value creation. In their comprehensive literature review, Zott et al. (2011) suggest that many define the *Business Models to emphasise a system-level, holistic approach to explaining how firms "do business"*; Osterwalder and Pigneur (2010) define a business model as "*the rationale of how an organisation creates, delivers, and captures value*".

Obviously, these features are broad and can be applied in a multitude of ways depending on what data available to assess the practicality of the concept used.

Using these describing features of a business model in banks, the following observations can be made:

1. A bank operates in a system where other banks compete to capture and create value;
2. By essence a bank is a regulated entity, this means that regulation impacts the choice and conduct of banking activities;
3. Banks' functions were defined in the literature as financial intermediation actors, maturity transformers, risk managers, information holders and innovators;
4. Banks take and manage risk via granting loans, investing and either holding or transferring the risk in the system on the assets side of its business, but also take and manage risk via collecting retail and market deposits and issuing short-term and long-term liabilities;
5. In the process of risk-taking and management of the assets and liabilities sides, the banks capture, deliver or destruct value. The value delivery is when a bank succeeds its role as a responsible (in terms of taking and managing risks) and sustainable (in terms of long-term contribution to the real economy) financial intermediation actor and hence contributes positively to the economy and society. The value destruction is when a bank fails its role and becomes on the contrary to what is its "raison d'être" toxic to the system. The level of toxicity is linked to the excessive risk taken that neither the bank nor the market can manage it effectively.

3.3.1 *Defining a Bank Business Model*

In view of the previous observations and after reviewing the infant literature on bank business models (see Box 3.1 on selected literature on bank business models), we propose a definition for a business model in a bank.

Box 3.1 Selected Literature on Bank Business Models

The literature on banking business models is still in its infancy. Indeed, its popularity took off after the GFC, in a view to renew the economic analysis of the behaviour or conduct of banks. Researchers have applied business model concepts to the banking industry in various ways. A selected review of the literature shows that there is growing interest on this topic by academics and policy institutions to identify and assess bank business models.

Following Ayadi et al. (2011) and subsequent research work on the topic, other researchers followed similar exercises using different set of indicators and using the clustering methodology. Ferstl et al. (2012) use a k-centroids clustering method based on the Mahalanobis distance in order to assigning 234 European banks to groups. Analysing the timeframe period from 2005 to 2011 of publicly available data from banks' financial statements, they use five variables to classify each bank: net interest income (as a percentage of operating income), trading income (as a percentage of operating income), income from fees and commissions (as a percentage of operating income), loan-to-deposit ratio and loans (as a percentage of total assets). They identified five different business models of banks and showed that banks adapted their business models after the crisis. Hryckiewicz and Kozłowski (2017) performed an analysis of the heterogeneity between different business models among systemically important banks in 65 countries over the timeframe of 2000–2012. The geographical coverage is the Americas, Europe and Asia. Using the k-medoid clustering approach, they identify four banking strategies, consisting in different combinations of bank asset and funding sources. They find that diversification does matter for banks since it helps them to reduce their individual risks. Their results show that investment model risk is difficult to detect because of a high level of off-balance sheet activities and derivatives not reported in the regulatory capital and that this model is the riskiest one. Traditional banks seem to be less risky than non-traditional counterparts. The study also shows that the asset structure of banks was

(*continued*)

Box 3.1 (continued)
responsible for the systemic risk before the mortgage crisis and that liability structure was responsible for the crisis itself. Tomkus (2014) has adopted a hierarchical clustering method inspired by the works of Ayadi et al. (2012) and Ayadi and de Groen (2014) to discriminate among business models. The dataset comprises 378 bank-year observations from 63 European and American banks spanning the years from 2007 to 2012. The paper identifies three distinctive business models: a wholesale-oriented universal banking business model, a retail banking business model and an investment banking business model. The study provides evidence that banks indeed change their business models as a reaction to changing environments and that bank migrations across business models is a phenomenon related to significant financial market events. Equally, Roengpitya et al. (2014) implement the clustering method of Ayadi and de Groen (2014) on the balance sheet data of 222 international banks over the years from 2005 to 2013, corresponding to 1299 bank-year observations. The coverage is 34 countries of Europe, North America, Asia, Oceania and emerging market economies. The study has identified three business models: a retail-funded commercial bank, a wholesale-funded commercial bank and a capital markets-oriented bank. One of their key findings is that banks engaging mainly in commercial activities have lower costs and more stable profits than those more heavily involved in capital market activities, namely trading. They also find that retail-funded banks engaging in traditional activities have gained in popularity over the past few years, because of their consistently stable performance. Roengpitya et al. (2017) applied a similar clustering methodology to a sample of 178 banks over 11 years (2005–2015). They examined the systematic effects that a bank's transition across business models over time may have on the bank's performance. They found that the retail-funded and wholesale-funded commercial banking models are more robust to the choice of inputs, compared to business models focused on trading activities and a universal banking model.

Other authors used other methods to identify business models in banks. Erins and Erina (2013) assessed the business models used by the five leading banks operating in each Central and Eastern Europe (CEE) country from 2006 to 2011. By using descriptive statistics to determine the constituent cluster components, they distinguish four different

(*continued*)

Box 3.1 (continued)

business model types: wholesale banks, investment banks, retail banks and universal banks. Basing their analysis of the data on indicators like Return on Assets (ROA) and Return on Equity (ROE), the authors conclude that the majority of the banks in the sample are universal banks. Jočienė (2015) attempts to identify the business models adopted by nine Scandinavian bank subsidiaries operating in the Baltic countries (Estonia, Latvia and Lithuania). The dataset comprises indicators of nine banks covering the period from 2006 to 2014. The methodology used is a combination of correlation analysis and simple linear regression. As a result, the main characteristics of the banks are elicited: retail banks operating in one jurisdiction, dependency on parent bank decisions, aversion to risk, stronger focus on non-interest income and high efficiency, orientation towards safety, medium profitability with a negative trend for the future. Curi et al. (2015) set out to determine the optimal business model of foreign banks operating in the financial centre of Luxembourg, before and after the financial crisis of 2007–2008. To this end, the paper investigates foreign banks' diversification through their asset mix, funding mix and income mix. The methodology is a combination of non-parametric tests, Data Envelopment Analysis, truncated regression and bootstrap. The results point to a focused asset, funding and income strategy as the most efficient business model and to the central role of the legal organisational status (subsidiaries or branches). Mergaerts and Vander Vennet (2016) use a panel of over 500 banks from 30 European countries over the period 1998–2013 to examine the impact of bank business model choices on their profitability, net interest margin and default risk. They conclude that, in the long run, a diversified income structure improves profitability without decreasing bank stability. Köhler (2015) examines the impact of business models on bank stability in 15 EU countries between 2002 and 2011. This empirical study draws on 25,996 bank-year observations of 3362 banks from the database Bankscope. The paper represents a business model of a bank by the share of non-interest income in total operating income and the share of non-deposit funding in total liabilities and uses bank balance sheet data. The paper provides evidence that banks would be significantly more stable and profitable if they increase their share of non-interest income, meaning that there are benefits to be gained from income diversification.

Source: Compilation of the author

In banks and other financial institutions, a pragmatic view of a business model is how these institutions manage their assets (activities) and liabilities (funding) over time to contribute to the financial system and the economy either by managing the risk (in their balance sheet and off-balance sheet or by accumulating it and transferring it to the system). The ultimate value captured can be a positive value when banks manage the risks over time and hence this value is delivered to the economy and negative when banks take excessive risks without being able to manage and hence produces negative externalities to the system leading to a destruction of value. Such destruction of value is detrimental to the economy and even more when taxpayers funded bailouts are allocated to limit the consequential effects of this value destruction.

The novelty of the **Activity-Funding (AF) definition** of a business model in banks or any similar institution borrows from this holistic system approach and applies it practically using the activity and funding profile of banks via their balance sheet and the asset-liability interaction over time.

The non-inclusion of off-balance sheet is due to the non-availability of reliable data.

For generalisation, the concept is referred at as BBM—bank business model using the Activity-Funding definition.

Elements of this definition were first introduced and tested on a small bank sample for the purpose of regulatory analysis in Ayadi et al. (2011, 2012) and later refined, completed, retested and generalised on larger bank datasets in Ayadi et al. (2016, 2017).

The definition emphasises the activities on the asset side and the funding on the liability side of the balance sheet of banks. It provides a holistic view as to how a bank behaves in the market while transforming its funding (retail, market (or wholesale) or mixed) into retail, market (wholesale) or both financing and investment opportunities (Fig. 3.1).

This approach is reflected in the assets and liabilities of a bank and how they interact at a point in time based on a given percentage of the categories of assets and liabilities. Each bank also interacts with other bank(s) via the liabilities and assets structure and their interaction. This determines the level of interconnectedness and complexity in the financial system.

3.3.2 Indicators Used in the A/F Definition

The following defining activity/funding features of a business model in banks in Europe from an asset and liability standpoint were used in the Ayadi and de Groen (2014) and Ayadi et al. (2016). These defining features result from data availability, statistical analysis, expert judgement and consultations.

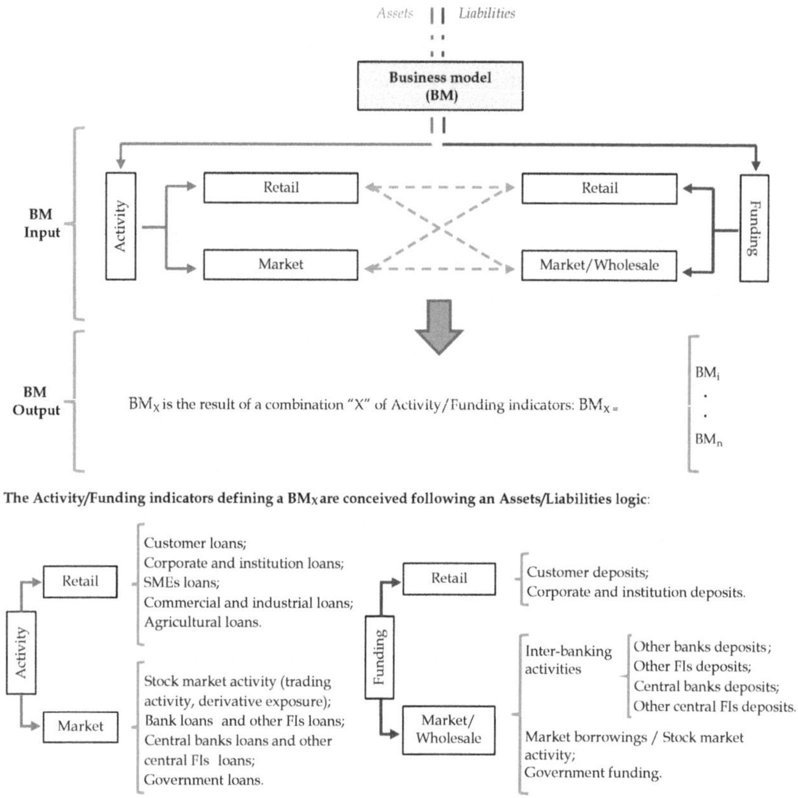

Fig. 3.1 Bank business model definition. Source: Author. Note: Market and retail activities and funding are broad categorisations used in this definition. Market and wholesale are used interchangeably

These features are first-level defining features of what a bank does (in terms of their assets side) and how it does it (in terms of the funding side).

On the asset side, three key defining features were identified:

Loans to banks (as % of assets). This indicator measures the scale of wholesale and interbank activities, which proxy for exposures to risks arising from interconnectedness in the banking sector.

Customer loans (as % of assets). This indicator identifies the share of customer loans to non-bank customers, indicating a reliance on more traditional banking activities.

Trading assets (as % of assets). These are defined as non-cash assets other than loans; a greater value would indicate the prevalence of investment activities that are prone to market and liquidity risks.

On the liability side, two additional defining features were identified:

Debt liabilities (as % of assets). These are defined as non-equity liabilities other than deposits and derivatives. Although bank liabilities are comprised of short-term interbank debt, the broader debt liabilities indicator provides a general insight into the bank's exposure to market funding. This indicator can be further broken down to the types of debt liabilities (e.g. short, medium to long term, and loans or market instruments) subject to data availability.

Customer deposits (as % of assets). The indicator identifies the share of deposits from non-bank/non-credit union customers, for example, households or enterprises, in the total balance sheet, indicating reliance on more traditional funding sources.

Derivative exposures (as % of assets).[1] This measure aggregates the carrying value of all negative derivative exposures of a bank, which are often identified as one of the key (and most risky) financial exposures of banks with heavy investment and trading activities.

This same list was used to define the BBM in Canada.

The list of instruments can be expanded depending on the availability of data on the structure of assets and liability collected. However, it is important that the same indicator is not providing the same information about the activity of a bank.

In Ayadi et al. (2017), the following seven instruments for banks and six instruments for credit unions in the US were used:

On the asset side, three key defining features were identified:

Loans to banks/credit unions (as % of assets). This indicator includes all loans other than those secured by real estate to deposit taking institutions (e.g. commercial banks, savings institutions, credit unions). Hence, this indicator measures the scale of interbank (inter-credit unions) activities,

[1] Total derivative exposures are defined as the summation of positive and negative fair values of all derivative transactions, including interest, currency, equity, OTC, hedge and trading derivatives.

which proxy for exposures to risks arising from interconnectedness in the banking and credit unions sectors.

Customer loans (as % of assets). This indicator identifies the share of customer loans to non-bank customers not held for sale, indicating a reliance on more traditional banking activities in the case of banks. The loans are netted from allowances for loan losses.

Trading assets (as % of assets). These are for banks defined as the book values of the total securities, loan and leases held for sale and other trading assets on the balance sheet,[2] while for credit union these include trading securities.[3] Large values would indicate the prevalence of investment activities, which are prone to market and liquidity risks.

On the liability side, two additional defining features were identified:

Bank/credit union liabilities (as % of assets). This indicator identifies the share of liabilities owed to other banks/credit unions, including deposits and issued debt. This may highlight banks/credit unions with greater interbank funding requirements, often due to an excessive reliance on short-term funding. This indicator includes all borrowings from deposit taking institutions (e.g. commercial banks, savings institutions, credit unions).

Customer deposits (as % of assets). The indicator identifies the share of deposits from non-bank/non-credit union customers, for example, households or enterprises, in the total balance sheet, indicating reliance on more traditional funding sources.

Derivative exposures (as % of assets). This measure aggregates the carrying value of all negative derivative exposures, which are often identified as one of the key (and most risky) financial exposures of banks/credit unions with substantial investment and trading activities.[4]

Debt liabilities (as % of assets). These are defined as demand notes issued to the US treasury, other borrowings and outstanding subordinated debt. The debt liabilities indicator provides a general insight into the bank's exposure to market funding. This instrument was not used for credit unions, since hardly any of the credit unions issues debt instruments.

[2]Accounting terminology uses a narrower definition of trading assets and would exclude securities/loans available for sale. The point of our clustering is to separate business models, so that 20% in "our trading assets" may fit as a non-trading bank and, since we are letting the data speak for itself, it might be 50% in "our trading assets" that makes banks a "wheeler-and-dealer" heavy trader type.

[3]Trading securities are securities that are held to be sold in the near future.

[4]For credit unions, the notional value has been used as the instrument for the clustering.

More indicators and defining features can be used depending on the level of granularity of data available under each of the five instruments chosen and beyond. It is very important to note that more granular data will allow a better understanding of business models in banking.

Indeed, the first-level features can be expanded if the types of activities (type of loans granted—to which sector, the different types of maturities, the different types of investment etc.) and type of funding (retail vs corporate or government depositors, between banks, from central banks, maturity of the funding etc.). The availability of this data allows more granularity of the bank business models and the ring fencing of risks based on very precise view on what banks do and how they take and manage the risk.

Moreover, this approach can be enhanced with the off-balance sheet indicators—however, the data is not available.

Other types of indicators can be studied and crossed with the BBM, such as ownership structure, level of internationalisation, systemic importance and size, which are not included in the definition of a BBM adopted.

The A/F definition is broad to include other assets/liability indicators (subject to data availability). It also allows comparability between banks and credit unions, and countries without having to include usually incomparable data of countries applying different regulatory frameworks and accounting standards in the same sample. It can be applicable to small and large samples and most importantly all institutions can be classified (e.g. performing and failing institutions). Moreover, this definition can be easily crossed with other assessment metrics, such as size, ownership, governance quality and other, and can be enlarged when more granular balance sheet data becomes available. The weakness of this definition is the non-inclusion of the off-balance sheet but if data is made available, the off-balance sheet data can be matched with the bank business models using the balance sheet data to assess the risk underpinning each business model.

To sum up, the business models analysis in banks has gained a great interest among scholars, analysts and regulators as a tool to classify banks and to better understand their performance and risk profiles. However, the business model concept remains ill defined.

This chapter reviews on the one hand the management and business literature that provided a starting point to understand the business model concept and the literature on banks on the other and proposes a definition of a business model in a bank using an **asset-liability approach** to define the activities and the funding profiles for a bank for **financial stability** purpose.

References

Achtenhagen, L., L. Melin, and L. Naldi (2013), "Dynamics of business models – strategizing, critical capabilities and activities for sustained value creation," *Long Range Planning*, 46(6), 427–442.

Ayadi, R., D.T. Llewelyn, R.H. Schmidt, E. Arbak and W.P. de Groen (2010), *Investigating Diversity in the Banking Sector in Europe: Key Developments, Performance and Role of Cooperative Banks*, Centre for European Policy Studies (CEPS), Brussels (https://www.ceps.eu/publications/investigating-diversity-banking-sector-europe-key-developments-performance-and-role).

Ayadi, R., R.H. Schmidt, S. Carbo Valverde, E. Arbak and F. Rodriguez Fernandez (2009), *Investigating Diversity in the Banking Sector in Europe: The Performance and Role of Savings Banks*, Centre for European Policy Studies (CEPS), Brussels (https://www.ceps.eu/publications/investigating-diversity-banking-sector-europe-performance-and-role-savings-banks).

Ayadi, R., E. Arbak and W.P. de Groen (2011), *Business Models in European Banking: A pre-and post-crisis screening*, Centre for European Policy Studies (CEPS), Brussels.

Ayadi, R., E. Arbak and W.P. de Groen (2012), *Regulation of European Banks and Business Models: Towards a new paradigm?*, Centre for European Policy Studies (CEPS), Brussels.

Ayadi, R. and W.P. de Groen (2014), "Banking Business Models Monitor 2014: Europe", Montreal, Joint Centre for European Policy Studies (CEPS) and International Observatory on Financial Service Cooperatives (IOFSC) publication (http://www.ceps.eu/book/banking-business-modelsmonitor-2014-europe).

Ayadi, R. et al. (2016), "Banking Business Models Monitor 2015: Europe", Montreal, International Research Centre On Cooperative Finance, HEC Montreal.

Ayadi, R. et al. (2017), " Bank and Credit Unions Business Models in the United States", Montreal, International Research Centre On Cooperative Finance, HEC Montreal.

Ayadi, R., Boussemart, J. P., Laleu, H., & Saidane, D. (2013). "Mergers and Acquisitions in European banking higher productivity or better synergy among business lines?". *Journal of Productivity Analysis*, 39(2), 165–175.

Baden-Fuller, C., and S. Haefliger (2013), "Business Models and Technological Innovation," *Long Range Planning*, 46(6), 419–426.

Bell, F. W., and N.B. Murphy (1968), "Economies of scale and division of labor in commercial banking." *Southern Economic Journal*, 131–139.

Benston, G. J. (1965), "Branch banking and economies of scale". *The Journal of Finance*, *20*(2), 312–331.

Benston, G. J., and C. W. Smith (1976), "A transactions cost approach to the theory of financial intermediation." *Journal of Finance*, 215–231.

Chesbrough, H. (2010), "Business model innovation: Opportunities and barriers," *Long Range Planning*, 43(2–3), 354–363.
Cull, R., Senbet, L., and M. Sorge (2004), Deposit Insurance and Bank Intermediation in the Long Run (No. 156). Bank for International Settlements.
Curi, C., A. Lozano-Vivas, and V. Zelenyuk (2015), "Foreign bank diversification and efficiency prior to and during the financial crisis: Does one business model fit all?," *Journal of Banking & Finance*.
Diamond, D.W. (1984), "Financial intermediation and delegated monitoring." *The Review of Economic Studies*, 51.3, 393–414.
Diamond, D. W., and P. H. Dybvig (1983), "Bank runs, deposit insurance, and liquidity". *The Journal of Political Economy*, 401–419.
Erins, I. U. and J. Erina (2013): "Bank Business Models and The Changes in CEE Countries." *World Academy of Science, Engineering and Technology*, Vol. 7 2013-03-28.
Ferstl, R., D. Seres, and K. Hornik (2012), "Clustering Austrian Banks" Business Models and Peer Groups in the European Banking Sector," *Financial Stability Report*, Issue 24, (December), 79–95.
Freixas, X., and J.C. Rochet (2008), *Microeconomics of Banking* (2e éd.), Cambridge, MA: MIT.
Gurley, J. G., Shaw, E.S., and A. C. Enthoven (1960), *Money in a Theory of Finance*. Washington, DC: Brookings Institution. Washington, DC: Brookings Institution.
Hryckiewicz, Aneta, and Lukasz Kozłowski (2017), "Banking business models and the extent of financial crisis." *Journal of International Money and Finance*, Vol. 71, No. C, pp. 1–24.
Jočienė, A. (2015), "Scandinavian bank subsidiaries in the Baltics: Have they all behaved in a similar way?." *Intellectual Economics* (2015).
Köhler, M. (2015), "Which banks are more risky? The impact of business models on bank stability," *Journal of Financial Stability*, 16, 195–212.
Leland, H. E., and D. H. Pyle (1977), "Informational Asymmetries, Financial Structure, and Financial Intermediation." *The Journal of Finance*, Vol. 32.2.
Magill, M., Quinzii, M., and J.C. Rochet (2015). "A Theory of the Stakeholder Corporation" *Econometrica*, *83*(5), 1685–1725.
Mergaerts, F., and R. Vander Vennet (2016), "Business Models and Their Impact on Bank Performance: A long-term perspective," *Journal of Financial Stability*, Vol. 22, issue C, 57–75.
Murray, J.D., and R.W. White (1980), "Economies of Scale and Deposit-Taking Financial Institutions in Canada: A Study of British Columbia Credit Unions," *Journal of Money, Credit and Banking*, 12(1), 58–70.
Osterwalder, A., Y. Pigneur, and C. L. Tucci. (2005), "Clarifying business models: Origins, present, and future of the concept." *Communications of the association for Information Systems*.

Osterwalder, A., & Pigneur, Y. (2010). *Business model generation: a handbook for visionaries, game changers, and challengers*. John Wiley & Sons.
Roengpitya, R., N. Tarashev, and K. Tsatsaronis (2014), "Bank business models," *BIS Quarterly Review*, (December), 55–65.
Roengpitya, R., Tarashev, N., Tsatsaronis, K., Villegas, A. (2017), Bank business models: popularity and performance, BIS Working Papers, No. 682.
Sealey, C. W., and J. T. Lindley (1977), Inputs, outputs, and a theory of production and cost at depository financial institutions. *The Journal of Finance, 32* (4), 1251–1266.
Teece, D.J. (2010), "Business Models, Business Strategy and Innovation," *Long Range Planning*, 43(2–3), 172–194.
Tomkus, M. (2014), "Identifying Business Models of Banks: Analysis of Biggest Banks from Europe and United States of America," Aarhus University. Retrieved from http://pure.au.dk/portal-asb-student/files/69715984/be_apendixu.pdf.
Zott, C., R. Amit, and L. Massa (2011), "The business model: Recent developments and future research," *Journal of Management*, 37(4), 1019–1042.

CHAPTER 4

Identification of Business Models

The bank business models (BBM) analysis relies on sufficiently granular, good quality and comparable data currently collected from the savings n loans (SNL) database. For several years, the author[1] led the research that developed several databases to test and analyse the concept of business models in banks and other financial institutions (e.g. credit unions) in Europe, US and Canada applying the **Activity/Funding (A/F)** definition proposed in the previous chapter. Earlier attempts of the BBM analysis were initiated to analyse how diverse is the banking sector in Europe[2] and the ongoing research is applying this approach to other countries.[3] This chapter describes the datasets and the methodology and shows the findings of bank business models (and credit unions) for Europe, the US and Canada.

4.1 Datasets and Samples Selection

The data collection and samples selection for Europe, US and Canada followed a progressive process of carefully assessing the data disclosed by banks in their annual reports and testing the concept of business models

[1] Ayadi et al. (2011, 2012, 2016, 2017) and Ayadi and de Groen (2014).

[2] The research on bank business models succeeded two research works on banking diversity in Europe, which assessed diversity via the co-existence between shareholder and stakeholders' banks (i.e. savings banks, public banks and financial cooperatives) (Ayadi et al. 2009, 2010).

[3] More research in ongoing to collect similar data for other countries subject to availability.

R. Ayadi, *Banking Business Models*, Palgrave Macmillan Studies in Banking and Financial Institutions,
https://doi.org/10.1007/978-3-030-02248-8_4

using elements of the definition we presented earlier. The process started with collecting data separately for Europe's banks, then later for the US and Canadians banks and credit unions to test whether the business model approach suggested is applicable and comparable between countries and different types of financial institutions where data is available (e.g. banks and credit unions). The choice of adding credit unions to the collection exercise was due to data availability on credit unions in the US but also to test the business model concept is applicable to other financial institutions other than banks. In Canada,[4] scattered data on credit unions is available, but more comprehensive data sets are available upon request.

The process of data collection followed *several steps*:

1. Careful examination of the annual reports of selected banks in Europe to better understand the balance sheet and income statements of the data disclosed; This first exercise was done in 2010 to screen the banking businesses and how they evolved before and after the great financial crisis;
2. Relevant balance sheet and income statements indicators were selected and redefined when definitions used by banks are not comparable;
3. Use of databases (e.g. SNL) to collect larger sets of data for the indicators selected for the generalisation of the business models analysis;
4. The data collection was done country by country to avoid any problems of comparability (e.g. between Europe, the US and Canada) due to different capital regulations and accounting rules;
5. Data for all samples is reviewed every year to enhance reliability and completeness of the datasets; and
6. Business models indicators for banks and credit unions are generated every year to ensure continuity.

4.1.1 Dataset for Europe

In Europe, the banking sector is diverse. It incorporates different institutional, organisational forms, business models and sizes. Apart from the very large-sized universal banks, which focus on a broad mix of banking activities, a large number of medium-sized banks offer retail or investment

[4] In Canada, the data on credit unions is not publically and easily available.

services. These institutions have different ownership structures, private, public, cooperatives and savings institutions. They all co-exist in this highly competitive diversified market.

To a large extent, the business models can be distinguished by the scope of activities and funding strategies they engage in or alternatively the breakdown of their income streams (e.g. interest income, trading income, commissions and fees and others).

Most retail-oriented banks, such as commercial, savings and cooperative banks, provide traditional banking services (e.g. payment services, retail and SMEs loans, investment activities) to the general public.[5] Investment-oriented banks focus more on trading activities, relying on a variety of funding sources and some of them are maintaining a retail network of their own. Other banks provide services to their institutional clients, including large and mid-sized corporations, real estate developers, international trade finance businesses, network institutions and other financial institutions and governments (e.g. public sector entities).

The first attempt to develop a database for banks business models in Europe was presented in the research[6] of (Ayadi et al. 2011), which included 26 large banks from Europe equivalent to 108 bank-year observations from 2006 to 2009. A qualitative assessment of these banks was done to better understand the business model of these institutions (see Appendix A for the list of the key balance sheet indicators to assess the business models of banks which were collected from yearly annual reports).

This exercise allowed to better understand the structure of balance sheet and the meaning of each indicator as reported by banks. This allowed to construct each indicator that contributes or not to the understanding of a business model in banks.

[5] Although most savings and cooperative institutions are local—leaving them outside the scope of this study—they nevertheless depend on the services of much larger central institutions, which typically provide their network institutions with liquidity and represent the group on a consolidated basis for supervisory purposes (Desrochers and Fischer 2005). Recent empirical work has shown that the local institutions have comparable performance and efficiency characteristics to their commercial peers and have largely weathered the financial crisis unscathed. However, a number of Spanish savings banks and the German central institutions have been hit hard. For more discussion on the European cooperative and savings banks, see Ayadi et al. (2009, 2010).

[6] This research was commissioned by the Greens—European Free Alliance Political Group in the European Parliament to understand how banks activities evolved pre and post great financial crisis.

The second attempt[7] presented in (Ayadi et al. 2012) enlarged the original sample to include 74 banks (up from 26 banks) with end-of-year data from 2006 to 2010, with 352 bank-year observations. This exercise was the first step in the testing and generalisation of the understanding of the "business model" of banks. In this exercise, only balance sheet instruments from the assets and liability sides were used in the identification of the business model of banks from a regulatory purpose. These variables are mainly bank liabilities, bank loans, debt liabilities, derivatives exposures and tangible common equity.

The third attempt[8] presented in (Ayadi and de Groen 2014) further enlarged the sample to include 147 large European Economic Area (EEA) banking groups and subsidiaries of non-EEA banking groups and included the EU-based cooperative banking groups and central institutions. The sample covered a list of balance sheet and income statement indicators for the years from 2006 to 2013 and includes 1126 bank-year observations. In this exercise, only balance sheet instruments from the assets and liability sides were used in the identification of the business model of banks. These variables are mainly bank liabilities, bank loans, debt liabilities, derivatives exposures, trading assets and customer deposits.

The fourth more comprehensive attempt[9] presented in (Ayadi et al. 2016) comprised 2542 banking groups and subsidiaries in the European Economic Area and Switzerland (CH).[10] This is equivalent to 13,406 bank-year observations, of which 13,040 have data for all instruments required to adhere to the business models framework. The increase is primarily due to the addition of many small banks and the increase in the geographical scope. The banking institutions are unequally spread across

[7] In a second study commissioned by the Greens-European Free Alliance Political Group in the European Parliament to advice on how bank business models can enhance the European regulatory framework on credit institutions—Mainly the Capital Requirements Directive IV and Capital Requirements Regulation (CRD IV—CRR) proposed by the European Commission in July 2011 that translates the Basel III standards adopted by the Basel Committee on Banking Supervision (BCBS) as part of the regulatory response to the great financial crisis.

[8] This research exercise was a result of collaboration between the Financial Institution and Prudential Policy (FIPP) at the Centre for European Policy Studies (CEPS) and the International Observatory on Financial Services Cooperatives at Hautes Etudes Commerciales (HEC) Montreal.

[9] This research exercise was conducted by the International Research Centre on Cooperative Finance of HEC Montreal, building on all the three previous research exercise on the topic.

[10] The sample includes the EEA+CH banking groups and banking subsidiaries of institutions from outside this region. The list of countries is in Appendix B.

the 32 countries in the EEA and Switzerland (see list of countries in Appendix B). More specifically, in the 19 countries of the Eurozone, 1859 institutions are considered, whereas in the nine non-Eurozone EU countries 334 institutions are covered. From the four EFTA countries (i.e. Switzerland, Norway, Iceland and Liechtenstein), in total, 349 banking groups and subsidiaries were included.

This database was gathered from private and public data sources by collecting accounting, market and other qualitative data building on the previous smaller databases. The database covered the period from 2005 to 2014. The balance sheet and profit and loss statement data were retrieved from SNL for more than 2500 banks, of which there has only been comprehensive coverage from 2010 onward. To improve the data entries before 2010 and limit the survivorship bias, the database was complemented with the data used in the third database (which included the 147 banks). To allow analysis on a bank group level, the immediate and ultimate owner data was complemented with information on the intermediate owner. Moreover, the database included further information on ownership structures, which made it possible to categorise banks in five broad structures as of 2014.

Further data was collected: the market data was obtained from Bloomberg and Markit, the asset quality review and stress test data for systemic banks from both the European Banking Authority (EBA) and the European Central Bank (ECB) websites. The estimates on the cumulative peak losses during the financial crisis for 62 banks have been obtained from De Groen and Gros (2015). In this exercise, the following assets and liabilities indicators were used to identify banks business models: bank loans, customer loans, debt liabilities, trading assets and derivative exposures. Indicators on bank activities, financial position, international activities, ownership, financial performance, risk factors, as well as regulatory indicators and supervisory measures, were constructed from this subset.

More recently (in 2017–2018), the database was reviewed, completed more comprehensively and is composed of 3287 banks of 32 European Economic Area and Switzerland. More specifically, in the 19 countries of the Eurozone, 2672 institutions are considered, whereas in the nine non-Eurozone countries we observe 357 banking institutions, finally, from the four EFTA countries (i.e. Switzerland, Iceland, Norway and Liechtenstein), in total 258 banking groups and subsidiaries were included. The sample covers more than 95% of the banking assets in the EEA. The sample includes 22,787 bank-year observations during the period that spans from

2005 up to 2016 (and currently being updated with data for 2017), covering both the period before and during the financial crisis and the recovery one. Data are collected from several data sources: bank specific variables are from SNL unlimited; macro-economic variables from the World Bank; state aid information are collected from the ECB and the European Commission database; corporate operations data (M&A) are collected from Zephyr database.

4.1.2 Dataset for the US

In the US, the banking sector incorporates a variety of business models, charter types and size ranges. Universal-type large commercial banks, with a focus on a broad mix of banking activities, co-exist with a large number of smaller specialised institutions known as community banks. In addition to the conventional commercial and savings banks, the sector includes cooperative institutions commonly known as credit unions (i.e. member-owned). Although these institutions do not have the same regulators as banks, they provide same banking services,[11] in particular loans and deposits to their members. Credit unions are regulated under a different regime than banks with, among others, different reporting requirements.

For banks, Ayadi et al. (2017) made the first attempt to construct a dataset for business models in the US. The database includes 10,352 commercial and savings institutions[12] active at least one or more years during the period from 2000 to 2014, corresponding to 98% of total assets of the industry (as of end year 2014). Bank holding companies and other types of holdings are not included in this sample. Overall, the banks sample comprises 108,226 bank-year observations. The balance sheet and income statement data were retrieved from the SNL database. The market data was obtained from Bloomberg.

For credit unions, the database includes 10,392 credit unions active during the period from 2000 to 2014 with 83% of total assets of the industry at the end of 2014. In total, 115,516 credit union-year observations were analysed. The dataset used was gathered from the database of the National Credit Union Administration (NCUA) and SNL.

[11] http://www.cuna.org/Research-And-Strategy/Credit-Union-Data-And-Statistics/.

[12] Savings institutions (also called thrift institutions, or thrifts) include savings banks, savings associations (formerly savings and loan associations) and cooperative banks.

4.1.3 Dataset for Canada

Finally in Canada, due to a dual banking system with federal regulators for banks and 11 provincial jurisdictions for credit unions and the Desjardins group (with its *Caisses populaires*[13]), the database covers a total of 59 institutions and includes 321 banks and credit unions—year observation accounting for 90% of total assets over a period of analysis 2010–2015. The data is collected from SNL database.

These databases are continuously reviewed, updated with the most recent available data from SNL and other data sources and used to produce the bank and credit unions business models for these countries and other countries where data is available and comparable.

The yearly results of the bank and credit unions business models computations will be available on the open access online platform (www.BBMresearch.org).

4.2 Methodology: Clustering

Clustering is a simple statistical technique used for assigning a set of observations (i.e. a particular bank or credit union in a particular year) to groups (i.e. business models as defined in this book) that do not generally overlap. By definition, observations that are assigned to the same cluster share a certain degree of similarity within the cluster, while being insufficiently dissimilar between themselves.

The preliminary step is the selection of the instruments (or variables used in the definition), as explained in the previous chapter. The selection of instruments depends on the definition of the business model adopted.

In our research work, the Activity-Funding definition following the asset-liability approach is adopted.[14] The clustering method itself includes a specification of the similarity or dissimilarity measure, the algorithm for recovering the clusters, and the determination of the appropriate number of clusters (i.e. the "stopping rule").

To form the clusters, Ward's (1963) **clustering procedure** to calculate the distance between clusters was used. The procedure forms partitions in a hierarchical manner, starting from the largest number of clusters possible (i.e. all bank/years in a separate cluster) and merging clusters by minimising

[13] No data available on the caisses populaires.

[14] Ayadi et al. (2011, 2012, 2016, 2017) and Ayadi and de Groen (2014).

the within-cluster sum-of-squared-errors for any given number of clusters. Several studies found that the Ward clustering methodology performs better than other clustering procedures for instruments that involve few outliers and in the presence of overlaps.[15]

For the US banking and credit unions sectors, a hybrid method combining the hierarchical Ward's (1963) procedure explained above and the non-hierarchical k-means algorithm is used to form the clusters.

The k-means algorithm allows observations to be reassigned across partitions during the iterations. The algorithm then proceeds by assigning each observation to the temporary cluster of the nearest centre. The new centre of a group is the average of the observations in that group. The process is iterated until the change in groups' centres becomes close to zero. The final clusters consist of the observations that are nearest to the centres in the last iteration.[16]

To diagnose the appropriate number of clusters, Calinski and Harabasz's (1974) pseudo-F index was used as the primary **"stopping rule"**. The index is a sample estimate of the ratio of between-cluster variance to within-cluster variance.[17] The configuration with the greatest pseudo-F value was chosen as the most distinct clustering. The results are confirmed under the Semi Partial R-Squared measure, the Cubic Clustering Criterion and the Sum of Squares Between measures (see Ayadi et al. 2016, 2017).

The clustering methodology is simple to apply to large and small-numbered observations' samples and easily reproduced by researchers

[15] See Milligan (1981) and references therein for an assessment of different clustering methods.

[16] The hybrid method, as applied to the two samples of US banks and credit unions, develops as follows:

Step 1: Perform a non-hierarchical algorithm; specify a very large number of groups (e.g. 500 groups)

Step 2: A hierarchical algorithm (Ward) is implemented by treating these 500 centroids as observations. This clustering will suggest taking Q groups

Step 3: Perform a non-hierarchical clustering with Q clusters using the Q centroids, found in the previous step, as the starting seeds.

Note that, for the success of the application of the hybrid method to this study, indicators, which are ratios, are not standardised as is common in the literature, because they are already dimensionless. In addition, standardisation results in clusters that are less intuitive to interpret.

[17] Evaluating a variety of cluster stopping rules, Milligan and Cooper (1985) single out the Calinski and Harabasz index as the best and most consistent rule, identifying the sought configurations correctly in over 90% of all cases in simulations.

who wish to reproduce the business models analysis using this definition or others as they may develop.

However, one of the key problems often encountered in clustering is the presence of missing values. When a particular observation has one or more missing instrument values, it has to be dropped from the cluster analysis, since the similarity to other bank-year observations cannot be determined. The samples used contain such cases, despite efforts to choose indicators with high coverage ratios. In order to accommodate the entire sample of observations in Europe, when the "intangible assets" and "negative carrying values of derivative exposures" were not reported, they were assumed to be zero in the calculation of **"Trading assets"**, **"Debt liabilities"** and **"Derivative exposures"**, since banks are not required to report both balance sheet items unless significant. For the US credit unions sample of observations, when the "derivative exposures" were not reported, they were assumed to be zero in the calculation of "Derivative exposures", since credit unions are not required to report the item when not applicable.

Nonetheless, the business model analysis—whatever the definition might be—remains dependent on methodological choices, including most notably the selection of indicators (which is linked to the definition used), clustering methodologies (static and dynamic) and procedures for forming clusters and the "stopping rule" used to determine the optimal number of clusters.[18] The instruments mentioned above led to the most consistent and distinct clustering. Dropping instruments resulted in a substantial worsening of the statistical measures of distinct clustering, whereas a larger set did not change the results substantially, as long as the defined indicators were included. Such experiments suggest that the chosen set of indicators, or instruments, adequately identifies the main distinguishing characteristics of the sampled banks and credit unions.

To conclude despite the methodological weaknesses, which can be overcome by testing other methods and definitions, the business models analysis remains a useful tool to understand what banks do and how they perform and contribute to risk in the system.

All the clustering procedures were conducted using SAS' built-in and user-contributed functions. The SAS codes are available to rerun the business models for banks and credit unions yearly and available upon request (www.BBMresearch.org).

[18] See Everitt et al. (2001) for an introduction to cluster analysis and some of the practical issues in the choice of technical procedures.

4.3 Business Models Identification

In what follows, the business models based on Activity-Funding definition are identified in Europe's banks, US banks and credit unions and Canadian banks and credit unions. The descriptive statistics are presented in Appendix C.

4.3.1 Business Models in Banks in Europe

Using the definition of business models suggested, the database to examine business models in banks in Europe (Ayadi et al. 2016) and applying the clustering methodology, the results show that the **pseudo-F indices** attain a single maximum, pointing to the five-cluster configuration as the most distinct one (see Table 4.1).

The interpretation of the results of the clustering (Appendix C) shows that banks in Europe operate using five business models, described as follows:

Focused retail banks provide traditional services, such as retail loans are funded by retail deposits.

Diversified retail (type 1) banks combine lending to retail with a moderate percentage of trading activities and primarily funded by retail deposits.

Diversified retail (type 2) banks lend to retail customers with a moderate percentage of trading activities using mainly market funding (i.e. debt liabilities) in addition to retail deposits.

Table 4.1 Pseudo-F indices for clustering configurations for banks in Europe

Number of clusters	*Pseudo-F index (Calinski and Harabasz)*	*Number of clusters*	*Pseudo-F index (Calinski and Harabasz)*
1	–	6	4798
2	4984	7	4723
3	4243	8	4783
4	4378	9	4699
5	5015	10	4602

Source: Reproduced from Ayadi et al. (2016)

Note: The Calinski and Harabasz (1974) pseudo-F index is an estimate of the between-cluster variance divided by within-cluster variance

Wholesale banks primarily engage in interbank lending and borrowing.

Investment banks are primarily engaged in trading and derivatives activities and funded with a mix of retail and market funding (Fig. 4.1).

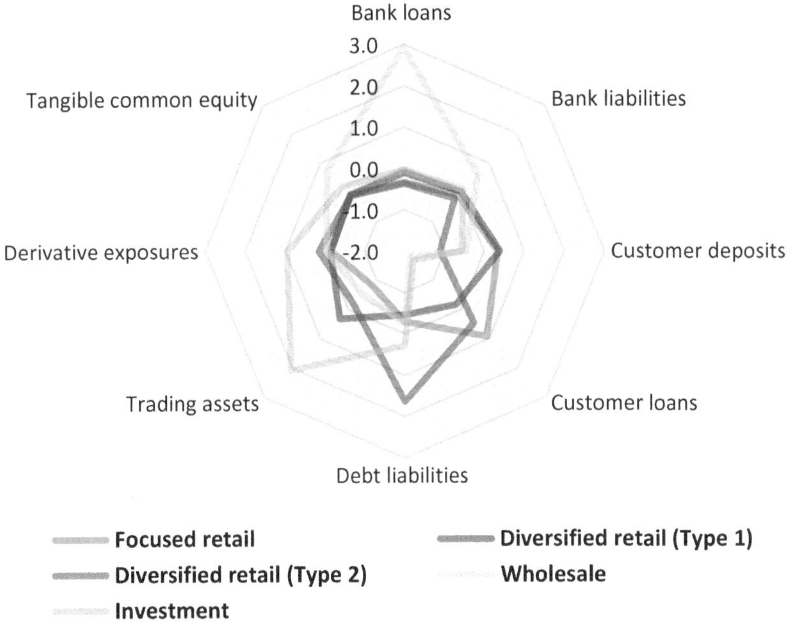

Fig. 4.1 Identification of bank business models in Europe, standardised scores. Source: Reproduced from Ayadi et al. (2016). Notes: Indicators marked with an asterisk (*) were used as instruments in the cluster analysis. The figures represent the number of standard deviations from the sample mean. *Customer loans* and *customer deposits* represent the balance sheet share of deposits from and loans to non-bank customers, respectively. *Bank liabilities* and *bank loans* identify the share of liabilities of and loans to other banks, including bank deposits, issued debt, interbank transactions and received funding from central banks. *Debt liabilities* are calculated by netting customer deposits, bank liabilities, total equity and negative fair values of all derivative transactions from total liabilities. *Derivative exposures* capture all negative carrying values of derivative exposures. *Trading assets* are defined as total assets minus liquid assets (cash and deposits at central bank) minus total loans and intangible assets. *Tangible common equity* is defined as common equity minus intangible assets and treasury shares as a share of tangible assets (i.e. total assets minus intangible assets)

4.3.2 *Business Models in Banks and Credit Unions in the US*

Using the databases examining business models in banks and credit unions in the US (Ayadi et al. 2017), the following procedure is used: a hybrid method combining the hierarchical Ward's (1963) procedure explained above and the non-hierarchical k-means algorithm is used to form the clusters.

To diagnose the appropriate number of clusters in Step 2, Calinski and Harabasz's (1974) pseudo-F index was used as the primary "stopping rule". The results for the bank sample show that the pseudo-F indices attain a single maximum, suggesting the four-cluster configuration as the most distinct one (see Table 4.2). For credit unions, the results show that a three-cluster configuration is the most distinct one (see Table 4.3).

The interpretation of the results of the clustering (Appendix C) shows that banks in the US operate using four business models (Fig. 4.2).

Table 4.2 Pseudo-F indices for bank clustering configurations in the US

Number of clusters	*Pseudo-F index (Calinski and Harabasz)*	*Number of clusters*	*Pseudo-F index (Calinski and Harabasz)*
1	–	6	53,000
2	54,000	7	50,000
3	57,000	8	48,000
4	**65,000**	9	47,000
5	57,000	10	47,000

Source: Reproduced from Ayadi et al. (2017)

Note: The Calinski and Harabasz (1974) pseudo-F index is an estimate of the between-cluster variance divided by within-cluster variance; the highest number is indicated in bold

Table 4.3 Pseudo-F indices for credit union clustering configurations in the US

Number of clusters	*Pseudo-F index (Calinski and Harabasz)*	*Number of clusters*	*Pseudo-F index (Calinski and Harabasz)*
1	–	6	10,000
2	11,000	7	9600
3	**12,000**	8	9200
4	11,000	9	8900
5	10,000	10	8800

Source: Reproduced from Ayadi et al. (2017)

Note: The Calinski and Harabasz (1974) pseudo-F index is an estimate of the between-cluster variance divided by within-cluster variance; the highest number is indicated in bold

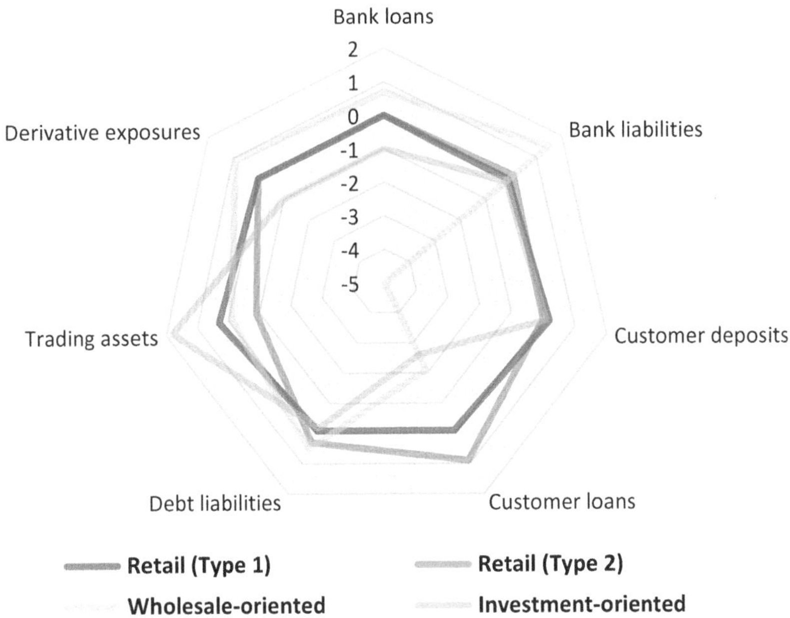

Fig. 4.2 Identification of bank business models in the US, standardised scores. Source: Reproduced from Ayadi et al. (2017). Notes: Indicators are those used for the clustering. The figures represent the number of standard deviations from the sample mean

Wholesale banks: These banks are active in the intermediation between banks, with a relatively heavy reliance on market/interbank lending and funding.

Retail banks type 1: These banks are active in lending to customers and show greater diversification in terms of investment activities and they use customer deposits as the primary means for funding.

Retail banks type 2: These banks are focused on retail activities. They are mainly active in lending to customers and they use customer deposits as the primary means for funding.

Investment banks: These banks are active in the trading activities and are predominantly funded by consumer deposits.

The interpretation of the results of the clustering (Appendix C) shows that credit unions in the US are active in three business models—all retail oriented (Fig. 4.3).

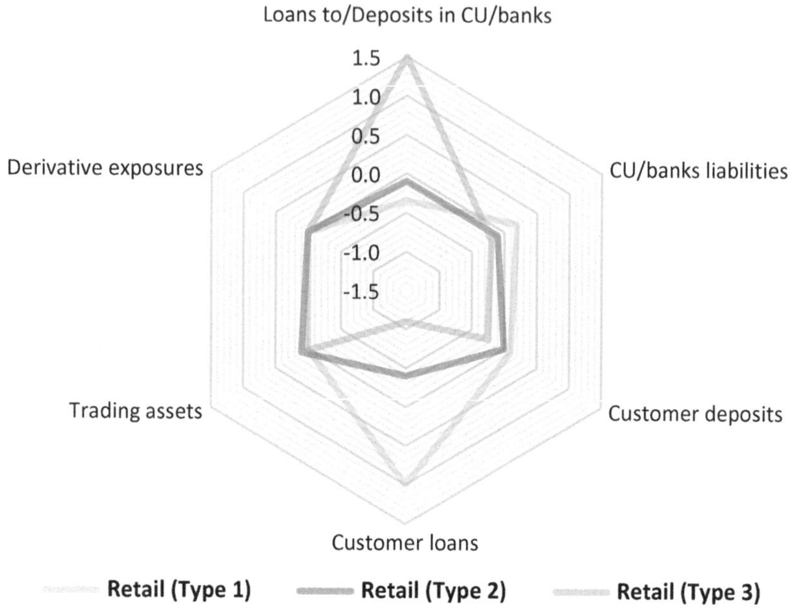

Fig. 4.3 Identification of credit union business models in the US, standardised scores. Source: Reproduced from Ayadi et al. (2017). Notes: The figures are the number of standard deviations from the sample mean

Retail type 1 credit unions *business models* are composed of credit unions that are focused on traditional deposit-loan intermediation. In particular, customer loans account on average for 71.35% of total assets, surpassing the sample average of 60.30%. On the liability side, these credit unions are largely funded via customer deposits.

Retail type 2 credit unions are more diversified between conventional deposit-loan intermediation, in particular, customer loans and depositing and lending to other credit institutions.

Retail type 3 credit unions primarily include institutions that are depositing or lending a larger share of their funds in/to other credit institutions. Indeed, on average, "interbank" deposit/lending activity represents nearly half of their balance sheet.

4.3.3 Business Models in Banks and Credit Unions in Canada

The same procedure applied and results show that the pseudo-F indices attain a single maximum, pointing to the three-cluster configuration as the most distinct one (see Table 4.4).

The interpretation of the results of the clustering (Appendix C) shows that banks and credit unions in Canada are active in three business models.

Diversified retail business models: These are institutions active in retail and investment activities and funded by a mix of retail and market funding;

Focused retail business models: These are institutions active in retail intermediation customer deposits and loans;

Investment-oriented business models: These are institutions that are active on trading and derivatives and mostly market funded (Fig. 4.4).

To conclude, this chapter identified the business models for comprehensive large datasets of banks and credit unions (when data is available) in Europe, US and Canada using the A/F definition and clustering methodology that is a simple statistical technique for assigning a set of observations into distinct group.

The results of the computations to identify business models in Europe, US and Canada show that:

- In Europe, there are five bank business models that include three retail oriented with different levels of activity diversification and funding mix and one investment and another wholesale oriented;

Table 4.4 Pseudo-F indices for clustering configurations in Canada

Number of clusters	*Pseudo-F index (Calinski and Harabasz)*	*Number of clusters*	*Pseudo-F index (Calinski and Harabasz)*
1	–	6	207
2	234	7	208
3	237	8	214
4	233	9	220
5	213	10	231

Source: Author

Note: The Calinski and Harabasz (1974) pseudo-F index is an estimate of the between-cluster variance divided by within-cluster variance

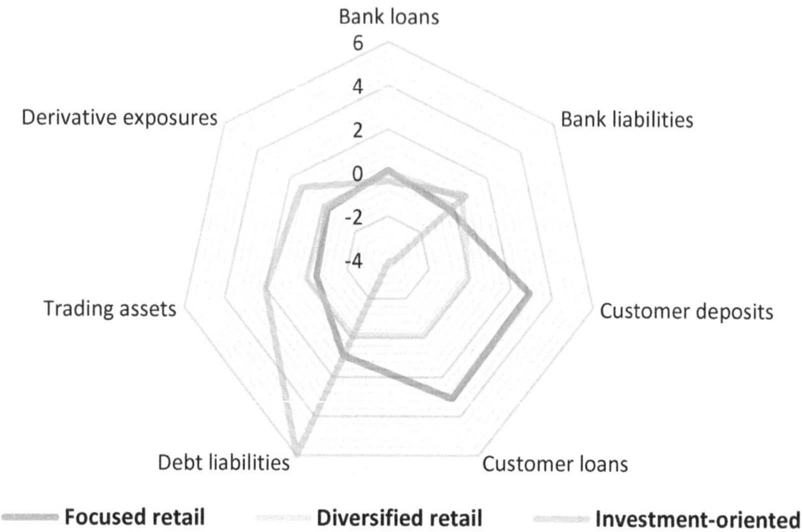

Fig. 4.4 Comparison of banks business models in Canada, standardised scores. Source: Author. Notes: Indicators marked with an asterisk (*) were used as instruments in the cluster analysis. The figures represent the number of standard deviations from the sample mean. *Customer loans* and *customer deposits* represent the balance sheet share of deposits from and loans to non-bank customers, respectively. *Bank liabilities* and *bank loans* identify the share of liabilities of and loans to other banks, including bank deposits, issued debt, interbank transactions and received funding from central banks. *Debt liabilities* are calculated by netting customer deposits, bank liabilities, total equity and negative fair values of all derivative transactions from total liabilities. *Derivative exposures* capture all negative carrying values of derivative exposures. *Trading assets* are defined as total assets minus liquid assets (cash and deposits at central bank) minus total loans and intangible assets. *Tangible common equity* is defined as common equity minus intangible assets and treasury shares as a share of tangible assets (i.e. total assets minus intangible assets)

- In the US, four bank business models that include two types of retail oriented, one investment and another wholesale and three types of retail-oriented credit unions with different levels of activity and funding;
- In Canada, three business models, two retail oriented with different level of diversification and one investment.

References

Ayadi, R., D.T. Llewelyn, R.H. Schmidt, E. Arbak and W.P. de Groen (2010), *Investigating Diversity in the Banking Sector in Europe: Key Developments, Performance and Role of Cooperative Banks*, Centre for European Policy Studies (CEPS), Brussels (https://www.ceps.eu/publications/investigating-diversity-banking-sector-europe-key-developments-performance-and-role).

Ayadi, R., R.H. Schmidt, S. Carbo Valverde, E. Arbak and F. Rodriguez Fernandez (2009), *Investigating Diversity in the Banking Sector in Europe: The Performance and Role of Savings Banks*, Centre for European Policy Studies (CEPS), Brussels (https://www.ceps.eu/publications/investigating-diversity-banking-sector-europe-performance-and-role-savings-banks).

Ayadi, R., E. Arbak and W.P. de Groen (2011), *Business Models in European Banking: A pre-and post-crisis screening*, Centre for European Policy Studies (CEPS), Brussels.

Ayadi, R., E. Arbak and W.P. de Groen (2012), *Regulation of European Banks and Business Models: Towards a new paradigm?*, Centre for European Policy Studies (CEPS), Brussels.

Ayadi, R. and W.P. de Groen (2014), "Banking Business Models Monitor 2014: Europe", Montreal, Joint Centre for European Policy Studies (CEPS) and International Observatory on Financial Service Cooperatives (IOFSC) publication (http://www.ceps.eu/book/banking-business-modelsmonitor-2014-europe).

Ayadi, R. et al. (2016), "Banking Business Models Monitor 2015: Europe", Montreal, International Research Centre on Cooperative Finance, HEC Montreal.

Ayadi, R. et al. (2017), "Bank and Credit Unions Business Models in the United States", Montreal, International Research Centre on Cooperative Finance, HEC Montreal.

Calinski, R.B. and J. Harabasz (1974), "A dendrite method for cluster analysis", *Communications in Statistics*, Vol. 3, No. 1, pp. 1–27.

Desrochers, M. and K.P. Fischer (2005), "The Power of Networks: Integration and Financial Cooperative Performance", *Annals of Public and Cooperative Economics*, Vol. 76, No. 3, pp. 307–354.

Everitt, B.S., S. Landau and M. Leese (2001), *Cluster Analysis*, Fourth Edition, West Sussex: Wiley, John & Sons Ltd.

Groen, W.P. de and D. Gros (2015), "Estimating the bridge financing needs of the Single Resolution Fund: How expensive is it to resolve a bank?", European Parliament, Brussels.

Milligan, G.W. (1981), "A Review of Monte Carlo Tests of Cluster Analysis", *Multivariate Behavioral Research*, Vol. 16, No. 3.

Milligan, G.W. and M.C. Cooper (1985), "An Examination of Procedures for Determining the Number of Clusters in a Data Set", *Psychometrika*, Vol. 50, No. 2, pp. 159–179.

Ward, J.H. (1963), "Hierarchical grouping to optimize objective function", *Journal of the American Statistical Association*, Vol. 58, No. 301, pp. 236–244.

CHAPTER 5

Bank Business Models and Financial Stability Assessment

After defining and identifying business models in banks in Europe, US and Canada, this chapter examines the relevance of the business models analysis in banking for **financial stability assessment**. First, it reviews the dimensions of financial stability and assessment framework broadly. Second, it explains how business models analysis in banks can serve to complete the **financial stability framework**. Third, it discusses the importance of the **business models analysis** for the future of **regulation** and **supervision**.

5.1 Financial Stability Assessment Framework

Financial stability is a fundamental policy objective but there is no single agreed definition for what it means to ensure its dimensions are dealt with by policy actions and tools.[1] Houben et al. (2004) define financial stability as "*a situation in which the financial system is capable of allocating resources efficiently between activities and across time, assessing and managing financial risks, and absorbing shocks*". According to the authors, a stable financial system is a system that "*enhances economic performance, and wealth accumulation, while it is able to present adverse disturbances from having an inordinate disruptive impact*". The authors also emphasise the dynamic

[1] For an overview of financial stability, see Houben et al. (2004).

R. Ayadi, *Banking Business Models*, Palgrave Macmillan Studies in Banking and Financial Institutions,
https://doi.org/10.1007/978-3-030-02248-8_5

nature of finance and hence financial stability and instability. In their framework definition, they interact several components of the financial system such as financial institutions, financial markets and infrastructure, which along their quest to perform their tasks in the economy, they contribute to stability and instability. The authors recognise the complexities underpinning this definition and the importance of public policy to ensure these complexities are understood, monitored and regulated to minimise instabilities during the cycle. Based on this definition, the authors propose a financial stability assessment framework building on the characteristics of finance. The objective of the framework is "*to foster an early identification of potential vulnerabilities, promote preventive and timely policies to avoid financial instability, and to resolve instabilities when preventive and remedial measures fail*".

In this framework of assessment, there are endogenous and exogenous factors that interact in the financial system (institutions, markets and infrastructure) and impact positively or negatively the economy. In the process, there are imbalances that ought to be corrected by preventive, remedial and resolution policy mechanisms. The operationalisation of the framework starts with analysis and monitoring, followed by assessment and policy actions using specific tools.

The authors treat financial institutions (e.g. banks, insurance companies, others) all together. When vulnerabilities start building up endogenously in one single institution or a group of institutions, they can spread to other parts of the financial system, in particular when other exogenous factors can interact to accelerate the instabilities. The sources of endogenous risks range of all types of risks financial institutions are supposed to manage (e.g. credit, operational, market, counterparty, reputational, liquidity, legal, concentration, business, governance).

For financial markets and infrastructure, other sources of vulnerabilities range from asset price misalignment to a run on a specific market or more broadly contagion.

To minimise the accumulation of vulnerabilities, preventive, remedial and resolution policy actions are taken. These actions range from regulation, supervision (micro- and macro-prudential), prompt corrective actions, to resolution and liquidation. For these actions to function, the timing of using each one of them is essential. But, to act timely, information must be available to be analysed for policy actions and tools to be fully functional and useful.

In 2012, Ayadi et al. (2012) urged for a fundamental rethink towards a **new conceptual framework** to achieve financial stability that considers all the costs and benefits of intervening in financial markets through micro- and macro-prudential regulations, supervision, monetary policy, crisis resolution and other institutional arrangements and structural reforms. According to this view, the conceptual framework applied to banks should be designed to fulfil two simultaneous objectives of the reform agenda, necessary for systemic financial stability:

1. To lower the probability of bank failures; and
2. To reduce the costs of those failures that do occur.

The first objective is linked to prevention and remedial regulatory actions, and the second objective is linked to resolution, liquidation actions and to the undesirable extreme case of the involvement of taxpayers in the form of bailout.

Theoretically, there is a trade-off between these two objectives in that the more the costs of failure can be reduced, the less intensive regulation needs to be to lower the probability of failure. When the arrangements for the resolution structures are determined and their application and level effectiveness are identified, the optimal intensity of regulation and structural changes can be defined for the benefit of financial stability. In practice, this is not easy to achieve because of the information asymmetry between banks and regulators due to the level of complexity and interconnectedness of today's banking and the potential risk of **regulatory capture**. If regulators cannot have a precise view on the business models of banks and their contribution to **accumulation of risks** in the financial system, and are unable to determine the timing and characteristics of a banking crisis before it occurs, then it is difficult to find an optimal mix between the two objectives. The lessons of the GFC showed that massive costly bailouts were engaged to keep the banking sector afloat in several countries without a precise knowledge of what the cost of failures of systemic banks in the global financial system would be and whether this cost of failures is higher or lower than what has been engaged globally using taxpayer-funded bailouts. These taxpayer-funded bailouts may have kept the global financial system afloat but reinforced the moral hazard problem in the system.

In their research, Ayadi et al. (2012) show that business models matter for the soundness of banks and overall to systemic stability and hence for the optimal design of banking regulation to restore incentives.

They recommend a complete rethink of the **one-size-fits-all regulatory paradigm** based on flawed Basel models and metrics (e.g. Tier 1 risk-weighted capital ratio) that determine the risks on the assets side of a bank but omit how banks get funded in the financial system and how leveraged a bank is and how this leverage evolves. They concluded that a new regulatory paradigm would require a better identification of business models and practices of banks and their evolution, and would systematically address their risks ex ante at any point in the economic cycle and ultimately their timely resolution, in case a crisis erupts.[2]

5.2 Bank Business Models and Financial Stability Assessment

When applying Houben et al.'s (2004) broad financial stability framework more specifically to banks and when applying the definition of a bank business model we propose in this book, there are endogenous factors that result from an overall risky business model of a single bank or a group of banks that can be profitable in the short run but, when interacting with other macro-economic and market factors, can create instabilities, in particular when preventive measures are flawed and/or weakly enforced. For example, banks that are active mainly in excessively risky short-term financial activities (and largely involved in credit derivatives to benefit from specific trade movements) and are being funded by short-term wholesale funding are much less resilient to a sudden market funding dry-up than banks that are focusing on retail activities and are funded by retail deposits and are not involved in trading complex financial instruments. Equally, banks that are active in mortgage lending and funded by retail deposits are much less resilient to a burst of a real estate bubble or an economic recession domestically than banks that are active in diversified market activities and funded in the wholesale market.

In the financial system, the net effect of the interaction of endogenous and exogenous factors on the business model of a bank, a group of banks and the financial system is very difficult to predict, particularly when the interconnectedness phenomenon is added to the picture.

To overcome this difficulty, relevant data availability and frequent monitoring of bank business models, for example, using the A/F definition,

[2] Later, Ayadi and Ferri (2016) showed that business models matter for the optimal design of banking resolution.

can become an essential policy tool for assessing the accumulation of risk per business model and managing it via regulatory, supervisory and resolution actions. This monitoring should also strive to understand how business models of banks (when defined and identified) interact with traditional metrics such as **size** and **ownership** and **organisational structures,** and whether and why business models change overtime and whether this change is beneficial or detrimental to the financial system. This monitoring exercise, therefore, allows a better understanding of how business models in banks evolve dynamically in terms of contributing to financial and economic performance, and contributing, accumulating and managing risks, and finally how they respond to regulation and ultimately resolution and liquidation based on the characteristics underpinning each business model. More broadly, a more informative assessment of **competition**, **concentration** and **diversity** in the banking market can be achieved when applying the business models analysis.

Bank business models, when identified based on an agreed definition, can be a policy tool in terms of prevention, remedy and resolution.

When the business models of banks are identified and the contribution to the systemic risk of each individual institution and a group of institutions is delimited based on different risk assessment metrics and methodologies, and when these business models are analysed in connection with other financial and macro-economic factors, then this analysis can provide additional information on how and to what extent a business model can be detrimental to excessive risk accumulation in the financial system or, on the contrary, conducive to a healthy risk allocation and risk management in the economy. This will determine whether there are sufficient regulatory backstops per business model when an external shock is hitting and how business models of institutions react to it.

Business models analysis for banks emerged in the capital regulatory framework in Europe only after the GFC[3] in 2013 and became one of the key elements of the **Supervisory Review and Evaluation Process** (SREP) although little is known about this concept. First, there has not been an

[3] DIRECTIVE 2013/36/EU OF THE EUROPEAN PARLIAMENT AND OF THE COUNCIL of 26 June 2013 on access to the activity of credit institutions and the prudential supervision of credit institutions and investment firms, amending Directive 2002/87/EC and repealing Directives 2006/48/EC and 2006/49/EC; and REGULATION (EU) No 575/2013 OF THE EUROPEAN PARLIAMENT AND OF THE COUNCIL of 26 June 2013 on prudential requirements for credit institutions and investment firms and amending Regulation (EU) No 648/2012.

official definition of what a business model is for a bank that is commonly adopted by the regulatory authorities and emerging research to adopt it in the regulatory framework. Despite this, in Europe, several competent authorities (e.g. the European Central Bank (ECB), the European Banking Authority (EBA) and several national central banks) and globally the Bank of International Settlements (BIS) engaged in identification and assessment exercises of bank business models based on the supervisory data available to them to better understand the intricacies of this concept and how it can be applicable for bank micro-prudential supervision. In other countries such as the US and Canada, the business model analysis is not formally enshrined in the regulation.

Adopting a common definition of a business model at a global or regional level will make the use of business models analysis in banks for regulatory purposes easier to apply to compare and better regulate banks in terms of micro-prudential policy for individual banks and in macro-prudential policy for a group of banks and the banking system as a whole.

The A/F definition we propose in this book and have tested for several years, several countries and datasets of different sizes allows for a comprehensive and comparable financial stability assessment as it takes into account the risks underpinned in the indicators used in the assets and liabilities of banks. Asset and liability are essential to understand the behaviour of a bank in the financial system, and when they interact they either create or destruct value. This definition allows for comparison between countries without having to include usually incomparable data of countries, applying different regulatory frameworks and accounting standards in the same sample. Moreover, the business model indicator produced using this definition can complement other assessment metrics such as size, ownership, governance quality and others, and can be enlarged when more granular balance sheet data and off-balance sheet data become available. The weakness of this definition is the non-inclusion of off-balance sheet data but if data is made available, the off-balance sheet data can be matched with the bank business models using the balance sheet data to assess the risk underpinning each business model.

We argue that the bank business models assessment framework can form part of the broader financial stability assessment framework that includes specifically the analysis of the interaction with size and ownership structure, migration of business models, economic performance, risk, resilience to external shocks, response to regulation and resolution. These are essential to understand the overall performance of a business model for a single bank, a group of banks and a banking system in a given country or a region.

This bank business models assessment framework can serve to assess the accumulation of risks over time and how regulation and ultimately resolution responds to it for individual banks and for a banking system as a whole. This makes the bank business models analysis a good tool for better regulatory prevention including micro- and macro-prudential regulation and resolution. This analysis is also relevant for the debate about proportionality that is essential to preserve a diverse banking system.

For **micro-prudential regulation**, when individual banks deviate from the average acceptable risk profile of a given business model and when the response of a bank or a group of banks under a specific business model to regulatory metrics is below what is expected, then a capital add-on can be computed under Pillar 2 of the Basel framework based on the additional risk incurred in the activities and funding profiles of these deviating banks. Applying more regulatory costs on these deviating banks will push back highly risky banks to the "healthy" references.

For **macro-prudential regulation**, when a group of banks in a country or a region with a risky business model are collectively increasing systemic risk, then an additional capital buffer should be applied to reduce the risk accumulation under that given business model—a capital buffer that is equivalent to the one designed for the large systemically important banks.

With time, and in the absence of **regulatory capture** and **forbearance**, a symmetric regulatory approach of capital requirement reduction can be applied for banks that operate under "healthy" business models. The capital reduction or capital discount can be further researched to ensure that its computation is carefully independently designed.

The business model analysis can prove useful for the debate on proportionality in bank regulation and structural reforms not only in Europe but also in the US and Canada. As a matter of fact, a large number of small and medium-sized banks, which were identified as predominantly retail-oriented institutions, seem to concentrate on traditional financial intermediation. There is a presumption that for these banks, the complexity of Basel regulation would drive compliance costs upward, which might in the long run hamper their prime role of financing the real economy. Further research on this matter is needed to make viable assertions. In turn, for large investment banks, which grew too complex and too large because of their market-oriented and international nature, the evidence shows that the worse-performing institutions might accelerate the accumulation of systemic risk and because of their rather weak resilience to extreme shocks, they could be subject to further bailouts if bail-ins under the resolution framework prove insufficient. For these latter cases, structural reforms (e.g. ring fencing or breakup) might prevent this risk from happening, although in the long run it is unclear whether this will be a viable solution.

For resolution, as was shown by Ayadi and Ferri (2016), calibrating the **Minimum Required Eligible Liabilities** (MREL) and the **Total Loss Absorption Capacity** (TLAC) to business models is essential to ensure that in the resolution phase there is no mi-calibration in terms of the risks related to the asset and liability structures of banks, which would be largely detrimental to the overall recovery of the financial system.

5.3 Bank Business Models and Restoring Basel Regulation Incentives

Ayadi (2012) provided a critical assessment of the evolution on the Basel global banking rules—the so-called Basel I, Basel II and Basel III over the last decades. She delved into how these rules impacted banks' incentives in particular via Basel II computation of the **risk-weighted assets (RWA)** central to the Basel II Tier 1 capital ratio and recommended for Pillar 2 to play a much central role in banking regulation instead of Pillar 1, which is mainly computed by banks themselves. In her paper, she emphasised that "*Pillar 1 should be viewed as complementing Pillar 2 to achieve effective supervision. Several indicators should be looked at under Pillar 1, including the Basel II risk sensitive ratio, a liquidity cushion and a leverage ratio.*" Along this same thinking and more critically, Ayadi et al. (2012) explicitly recommended a complete rethink of the one-size-fits-all regulatory paradigm based on the flawed Basel metrics (e.g. Tier 1 risk-weighted capital ratio) by requiring a better identification of business models and practices of banks and their evolution that would systematically address their risks ex ante at any point in the economic cycle.

Assuming there is no regulatory forbearance and no regulatory capture, for supervisors to have power over regulating banks credibly, there should be a coherent policy tool to allow them to better understand what banks do in practice based on their role in the financial system. Relying on banks' self-measured risk metrics such as RWA might not be enough for supervisors to have a well-informed view on what banks do and what their interactions with other institutions in the markets and in different countries are and above all what their incentives are when they make their trades.

The bank business model approach is useful as a regulatory tool to regulate banks and their underlying incentives. It will help overcome the weakness of regulating banks using a one-size-fits-all approach of Basel by reducing the asymmetry of information between banks and regulators and hence apply the right amount of capital, leverage and liquidity requirements needed based on the role of banks in the economy over time.

Once the business models in banks are identified using a commonly accepted definition and the evolution from one business model to another is explained, then their contribution to the accumulation of risk in the financial system and their role in the economy are better assessed. Having this policy tool to monitor the behaviour of banks will allow regulators to better regulate and supervise using either micro-prudential or macro-prudential tools calibrated to the banks business model. The new regulatory framework design that is calibrated to the bank business models is developed in such a way that the banks deviating from what is to be considered a "healthy state under a business model" should be either rewarded or penalised depending on the sign of the deviation (i.e. contributing to less risk of more risk). To achieve this, more research must be done to understand what is a healthy state (or states) under a business model and how it relates to the economic cycle and allocation of capital in the economy.

The expectation is that in principle, banks would have lower incentives to cheat the regulatory (and resolution) system that is calibrated to their business model because the information about their business model is known to their regulators and can be used as additional market information and updated over time and hence the level of capital, leverage and liquidity in the financial system will tend to be at the optimal levels. In the long run, this will lead to more efficient allocation of capital and liquidity in the economy.

To conclude, this chapter explained how the business models analysis could form part of the financial stability assessment framework and could serve as a policy tool in terms of prevention, remedy and resolution.

The business model assessment framework includes how business models interact with other traditional metrics such as size, ownership and organisational structure, the determinants of business models migration and contribution to systemic risk, how business models contribute to financial and economic performance, how they accumulate and manage risks and how they respond to regulation and resolution.

In the chapters that follow, we present the bank business models assessment framework for Europe, US and Canada.

References

Ayadi, R., E. Arbak and W.P. de Groen (2012), *Regulation of European Banks and Business Models: Towards a new paradigm?*, Centre for European Policy Studies (CEPS), Brussels.

Ayadi, R. (2012), on Basel regulation and banks' incentives, in New paradigms in banking, financial markets and regulation, Edited by Morten Balling, Frank Lierman, Freddy Van den Spiegel, Rym Ayadi & David T. Llewellyn, SUERF Study2012/2, Larcier.

Ayadi, R and G. Ferri (2016), Total Assets versus RWA: does it matter for MREL requirements, European Parliament, Brussels.

Houben, A., J. Kakes and G. Schinasi (2004), Toward a framework for safeguarding financial stability, IMF Working Paper 04/101, IMF, Washington, DC.

CHAPTER 6

Business Models, Ownership, Organisational Structures and Size

The bank business models analysis complements the traditional ownership, organisational structure and size analyses.

Ownership is fundamental to understand the underlying incentive of a financial institution. When the incentive is solely profit maximising, then institutions tend to take additional risk while minimising all other costs. When the incentives differ from this market "reference", then distinctions become blurry and more research is needed to understand these incentives and how they evolve in the financial system.

Organisational structure is another important dimension to assess banks in particular when the internationalisation strategy (e.g. via subsidiaries, branches or both) is involved.

Assessing **size** in economic theory applied to banking has targeted the finding of the optimal size. However, the size concept has also pre-empted the "too big to fail" concept and has been used by the international regulatory authorities to list the systemically important financial institutions worldwide.

This chapter examines the interaction between business models and ownership and organisational structures in banks in Europe on the one hand and the interaction between business models and size in banks in the US on the other hand. In Europe, there is large diversity in ownership structures. In the US, size has been a key dimension in categorising banks. This chapter finally provides a brief assessment of the Canadian banking sector.

R. Ayadi, *Banking Business Models*, Palgrave Macmillan
Studies in Banking and Financial Institutions,
https://doi.org/10.1007/978-3-030-02248-8_6

6.1 Business Models, Ownership and Organisational Structure and Size

Understanding the interaction between business models, ownership, organisational and size dimensions in banks and other financial institutions is important to better assess systemic risk and better analyse financial stability conditions and what causes instability.

Ownership structure defines who owns the financial institution and hence determines the underlying incentives of an institution. Shareholders-owned financial institutions are generally profit maximising while stakeholders-oriented financial institutions tend to fulfil stakeholders' objectives (e.g. cooperatives and mutual financial institutions claim to maximise members' surplus and savings banks owned by foundations tend to pursue their missions). The attitudes to risk-taking differ when incentives are different from profit maximisation. Generally, profit-maximising financial institutions tend to take more risk to maximise profit and generate high dividends for their shareholders to invest more in equity. Such an incentive leads to high profitability and more risk-taking over time. If this risk is not managed adequately, then unmanaged excessive risk can cost dearly to the financial system and to the economy and society as a whole. Other institutions may not be profit-maximising institutions because of their underlying institutional setting but they have clear mandates to enhance financial access and/or to maximise their members' surplus (via subsidies in financial services pricing or whatever this surplus means (e.g. distribution of vouchers or discounts on financial services)). Such an incentive may also lead to excessive risk-taking in particular when institutions are not subjected to market discipline. A careful understanding of the risk accumulation profile of each ownership structure is essential to better understand its contribution to the risk accumulation in the overall financial system.

Organisational structure defines how an institution is organised domestically and across borders via branches or subsidiaries or both. This reflects the internationalisation strategy of a bank but also how it is organised when it goes across borders. When a bank is headquartered in a country, it is supposedly regulated and supervised in the home country and can operate via branches and subsidiaries when it goes international. The branches are under home supervision and subsidiaries are under host supervision. Organising via branches or subsidiaries has implications for the risks domestically and across borders, and raises issues of cross-border coordination and exchange of information between supervisors. In a crisis situation, this is essential and raises political economy aspects.

Size is another important dimension that defines the importance of financial institutions (e.g. total assets, credits and deposits) relative to the gross domestic product (GDP) of a country or a region. Size also determines whether a financial institution is or not systemically important domestically, regionally or globally. Size is also an important factor to determine whether an institution is "too big to fail" or "too big to be unwound" and whether a structural reform is the preferred avenue to break up to reduce the moral hazard relative to size.

The risk profile and the contribution to systemic risk of a financial institution that is small, retail oriented and domestic are different from those of a financial institution that is large, investment oriented and international.

This difference in risk profile and risk accumulation over time per business model in the financial system requires a comprehensive financial stability assessment framework that includes:

1. assessment and management of risks relative to size;
2. assessment and management of risks relative to ownership structure;
3. assessment and management of risks relative to organisational structure;
4. assessment and management of risks relative to business models;
5. assessment and management of risks relative to the interaction of size, ownership structure, organisational structure and business models.

6.2 Business Models and Ownership Structures of Banks in Europe

Europe is home to large diversity in banking in terms of ownership, organisational structures, size and business models. The financial integration process, which contributed to this diversity, was made possible thanks to the 1999 Financial Services Action Plan (FSAP). This process allowed several banks to internationalise across their original boarders via single passporting, a consolidation process that resulted in the emergence of large cross-border financial groups that operate in several European countries either via branches or subsidiaries or both with no restriction.[1] Smaller and local groups (e.g. such as local savings banks and cooperatives) have remained confined to their original boarders, while the medium-sized institutions have chosen to internationalise by acquiring banks in other countries, particularly in Eastern Europe during the European enlargement period.

Looking at the ownership structure, in the banking sector in Europe, a distinction can be made between shareholder-value (SHV) and stakeholder-value (STV) banks. The co-existence of these two structures determines the extent of institutional diversity in the sector.[2] The main objective of the SHV banks is to maximise profit to the shareholders (or equity holders), while the STV banks have multiple objectives (e.g. maximise the surplus of members for cooperatives and similar institutions while making profit). Hence, these institutions qualify as "dual or multi bottom-line" institutions that have the combined profit-making for the banks' financial viability and adding value for their stakeholders—whatever this value means. However, the objectives—other than profit maximisation—can be too broad and may not be easily assessed and monitored. All institutions (SHV and STV) use the profitability metrics to assess their performance, which makes the distinction between the two difficult to make. A more informed distinction should use other metrics to understand how STV institutions benefit the economy and the society beyond profits.

In the dataset for Europe, the key characteristics of the different ownership structures[3] are described below as in Ayadi et al. (2016):

Commercial banks (SHV). These banks take many different forms, but have in common that they are in general privately owned by their shareholders and are driven by profit maximisation to satisfy the dividend expectations of their shareholders. The commercial banks include banking groups as well as subsidiaries owned by non-EEA and CH entities.

Cooperative banks (STV). There are large differences between cooperative banks in Europe, which do not make it easy to place these institutions under a single definition.[4] But, in general, the main distinguishing characteristic is that cooperative banks belong to their members who have equal voting power (one member one vote) and are entitled to the nominal value of the shares. These shares are generally dispersed and members

[1] Ayadi and Pujals (2005).

[2] See Ayadi et al. (2009, 2010) for an extensive analysis on institutional diversity in banking in Europe.

[3] The type of ownership structure is determined based on the situation of the banking group during the summer of 2015.

[4] For a comprehensive account on cooperative banking in Europe, see Ayadi et al. (2010).

have little to no disciplinary power on the management of the bank. Moreover, the central institutions that are owned by the member-owned banks and are not reporting consolidated financial figures are also recognised as cooperative banks and can operate unilaterally from the members' organisations.

Nationalised banks (SHV). During the financial and economic crises in Europe, governments intervened to safeguard financial stability. Support came in the form of recapitalisations, asset relief measures, loans and guarantees. In return, the governments received fees and, in some cases, also shares. In cases where a government obtained control (i.e. more than 50% of the shares) and kept it for a few years (at least until the summer of 2015), the bank was considered as being nationalised. The nationalised banks are either prepared to become commercial banks or are being liquidated. These banks are value maximising under the conditions agreed to in their nationalisation.

Public banks (STV). Some public bodies (e.g. local-, regional-, central governments) also have banks to support them in fulfilling their public interest objectives. Hence, most of these banks raise funds and provide financing for the activities of public bodies.

Savings banks (STV). The savings banks in Europe have many different characteristics; they can be owned by public bodies or foundations,[5] but have in common that they originally focused on providing access to financial services for the less wealthy amongst the population. Like the cooperative banks, the savings banks are in many cases supported by central institutions. In cases where the local savings banks and central institutions were not reporting consolidated financial figures, the central institutions are nevertheless recognised as savings banks. The savings banks are considered STV.

The descriptive statistics for the main variables describing the activities and funding strategies across ownership structures are provided in Appendix C.

One key observation that emerges from Table 6.1 is that, based on the bank-year observations during the whole period, all ownership structures operate in the five business models as defined in this book following different percentages.

In terms of number of institutions, wholesale and investment banks are mostly SHV banks, while retail banks are mostly STV banks, which is reflected in the highest share of cooperative and savings banks in the

[5] For a comprehensive account on savings banks in Europe, see Ayadi et al. (2009).

Table 6.1 Ownership attributes of business models (% of institutions)

	Model 1—Focused retail (%)	*Model 2—Diversified retail (type 1) (%)*	*Model 3—Diversified retail (type 2) (%)*	*Model 4—Wholesale (%)*	*Model 5—Investment (%)*	*All (%)*
Commercial	23.9***	18.3****	26.7***	73.1****	55.2****	28.4
Nationalised	1.0**	1.6***	5.4****	0.1***	3.1****	2.0
Shareholder value	24.9****	19.9****	32.1****	73.2****	58.3****	30.4
Cooperative	39.3****	48.6***	45.4***	11.5****	23.7****	40.5
Savings	30.6***	30.7***	16.8***	8.3****	15.4***	25.6
Public	5.2**	0.8****	5.6**	7.0**	2.6****	3.5
Stakeholder value	75.1****	80.1****	67.9****	26.8****	41.7****	69.6
Listed on stock exchange	12.7***	8.3****	21.9****	4.0****	14.8***	12.0

Source: Reproduced from Ayadi et al. (2016)

Notes: All figures are the average values for the year-end observations for the business models. The independence of cluster sub-samples was tested using the Wilcoxon-Mann-Whitney non-parametric two-sample tests at 5% significance. According to the results of these tests, the number of asterisks (*, **, *** or ****) stands for the statistical difference of any given cluster from that of other clusters for that indicator. Also, see in footnote 9 the precision about data on ownership structure sample. Moreover, a relatively large share of the wholesale banks has public ownership, which is also reflected in the share of public listings. Moreover, the highest share of listed banks can be found among the diversified retail (type 2) banks. In terms of total assets, the same observation is confirmed; commercial banks are, on average, more active in investment and less in retail activities than other ownership structures, while cooperative and savings banks are relatively more retail oriented.

This pattern should be monitored frequently to understand the risks underlying the evolution of the business models of the different ownership structures in Europe.

In terms of the organisational structure, which reflects the internationalisation strategy, investment banks are the most internationally active among retail and wholesale banks.

Table 6.2 shows that the average banks in this model have credit institutions and/or branches in more than six European countries. This is significantly more than that of wholesale and retail-focused banks, which cover between one and two countries. Both types of diversified retail banks have international activities. The average investment and diversified retail (type 2) banks also have more than one subsidiary, which is often used to conduct more substantial international activities. The average investment bank has 3.6 subsidiaries, while the average diversified retail bank has one.

The SHV banks are significantly more internationally active than STV banks, which remain domestically oriented. Hence, the commercial and nationalised banks are active in 2.3 and 4.2 countries, respectively, whereas the other banks are only, almost exclusively, active in their home markets. The figures for the cooperative and savings banks need to be interpreted carefully. In fact, the international activities of these banks are often exclusively performed by the central institutions within a network of banks. These central institutions of cooperative groups can also operate as investment banks.

This pattern should be monitored frequently to understand how banks business models change their internationalisation strategy.

6.3 Business Models and Size of Banks in the US

In the US, regulators and supervisors such as the Federal Reserve (Fed) and the Federal Deposit Insurance Corporation (FDIC) use different classifications for both individual banks and holding companies that can be adjusted over time. The US banking sector features a wide range of banks,

Table 6.2 International activities

(a) Business models

	Model 1—Focused retail	*Model 2—Diversified retail (type 1)*	*Model 3—Diversified retail (type 2)*	*Model 4—Wholesale*	*Model 5—Investment*	*All*
International activities (number of unique EEA countries)	1.5***	2.6***	3.8**	1.9*	6.4***	1.6
Internationalisation through subsidiaries (number of unique EEA countries)	0.3**	0.8**	1.2***	0.3*	3.6****	0.3
Internationalisation through branches (number of unique EEA countries)	0.2***	0.8***	1.6**	0.6	1.9**	0.3

(b) Ownership structures

	Commercial	*Cooperative*	*Nationalised*	*Public*	*Savings*	*All*
International activities (number of unique EEA countries)	2.3****	1.2****	4.2****	1.1***	1.2***	1.6
Internationalisation through subsidiaries (number of unique EEA countries)	0.5****	0.1****	1.8****	0.1****	0.1****	0.3
Internationalisation through branches (number of unique EEA countries)	0.7****	0.1***	1.5****	0.0***	0.1****	0.3

Source: Reproduced from Ayadi et al. (2016)

Notes: Number of unique EEA countries in which the bank had banking activities at year end of 2012, that is, parent institution, subsidiaries and branches with credit institution licence or passport. All figures are the average values for the year-end observations for the business model or ownership structure. The independence of cluster sub-samples was tested using the Wilcoxon-Mann-Whitney non-parametric two-sample tests at 5% significance. According to the results of these tests, the number of asterisks (*, **, ***, or ****) stands for the statistical difference of any given cluster from that of other clusters for that indicator from the generally considered small community banks (with total assets of less than $10 bn) to mid-sized regional banks (between $10 bn and $50 bn) and large national and global banks (more than $50 bn). Each category of bank has a role to play in the financial system, for example, serving retail customers, SMEs, larger companies, governments and so on.

About 98.8% of the banks[6] in the sample have $10 bn or less in total assets. In terms of the share of total assets, this category of banks is, nevertheless, responsible for only 22.5%. This category has been split into three size categories—namely banks with less than $1 bn, between $1 bn and $5 bn, and between $5 bn and $10 bn—to better understand the size dimension.

Appendix C provides descriptive statistics for these banks across the five categories of size for the overall period of analysis (2000–2014).

As described in Ayadi et al. (2017), the characteristics of US banks of different sizes are as follows:

The **micro-sized banks** include institutions with less than $1 bn in total assets, covering almost 90% of the observations, which makes it the largest size category of banks in the sample, but it accounts for only 11% of total assets. The average size of these banks is just about $180 mn. They are mostly retail type 2 banks active in traditional deposit-loan intermediation with customer loans and deposits of 63.81% and 80.25%, respectively, and relatively below the sample average of market and interbank activities.

The **very small-sized** banks include institutions with between $1 bn and $5 bn in total assets. These account for around 5.2% of the number of observations and 7.2% of the total assets and are, therefore, larger than the previous size category, with an average of $2 bn in total assets. In terms of the business model, these banks are fairly similar to micro-sized banks. Customer loans are lower (63.34%), a smaller share of funding is obtained from customer deposits (74.15%) and a higher share from debt liabilities (7.22% compared to 4.89% for micro-sized banks).

The **small-sized banks** include banks with between $5 bn and $10 bn in total assets. These banks represent 0.8% of the total observations and 3.8% of the total assets, with an average bank size of $7 bn. The composition of the assets is similar to those of micro-sized banks. The main items, customer loans (60.54%) and trading assets (24.02%), are not significantly different. In turn, a larger share of funding is obtained from market sources, with debt liabilities considerably higher than those of both previous size categories, while their customer deposits (of 65.67%) rank below those of both categories.

[6] So-called community banks include both commercial banks and savings institutions.

The **mid-sized** category includes banks with assets between $10 and $50 bn. Although the number of observations is comparable to the small-sized banks (0.8%), the share in total assets amounts to 12.2%. The composition of the assets is comparable to that of the third size category, while liabilities are less reliant on customer deposits. Indeed, with this size category, the decrease in reliance on customer deposits and the increase in reliance on debt liabilities continue. But the debt liabilities of 12.54% are not significantly different from those for small-sized banks.

The **large category** includes banks with more than $50 bn of assets (with an average size of $250 bn). They are the smallest in number, but control the majority of the assets. These banks represent only 0.4% in number but 65.3% in total assets. They are significantly less active in traditional deposit-loan intermediation, with customer loans (48.4%) and deposits (51.33%) being well below the sample average, while active in market-based activities.

Turning to the distribution of the various size categories across business models in terms of number of observations, it is clear that all bank sizes operate in the four business models defined in this book. Table 6.3

Table 6.3 Size attributes of bank business models (% of observations)

Amount in USD	*Model 1—Wholesale oriented (%)*	*Model 2—Retail (type 1) (%)*	*Model 3—Retail (type 2) (%)*	*Model 4—Investment oriented (%)*	*All (%)*
Micro (<1 bn)	86.5***	89.8*	88.3*	91.5*	89.3
Very small (1–5 bn)	5.6**	7.3***	8.2**	5.6***	7.3
Small (5–10 bn)	3.5***	1.4*	1.7*	1.4*	1.6
Mid (10–50 bn)	2.6***	1.2***	1.4***	1.2***	1.3
Large (>50 bn)	1.8***	0.3*	0.4*	0.3*	0.4

Source: Reproduced from Ayadi et al. (2017)

Notes: All figures are average values of the year-end observations. The independence of cluster sub-samples in each size category was tested using the Wilcoxon-Mann-Whitney non-parametric two-sample tests at 5% significance. To report the results of these tests, the number of asterisks (*, **, or ***) stands for the statistical difference of any given cluster from that of other clusters in the size category. For example, two asterisks (**) imply that the cluster is statistically different from two other size categories but not the third and fourth (closest) ones shows that the large majority of institutions are micro-sized banks (between 86.5% and 91.5% across business models). As for the remaining categories, the very small institutions are relatively more represented in the retail type 1 and type 2 business models, while small, mid-sized and large banks are relatively more represented in the wholesale-oriented business model.

6.4 Business Models, Size and Ownership of Banks in the Canada

In Canada, the banking sector is much smaller than those in Europe and the US. Banks are regulated by the federal regulator and credit unions and the Desjardins group (with its *Caisses populaires*) are regulated by the 11 provincial jurisdictions.

Traditionally, regulation has imposed more restrictions on the ownership and activities of foreign banks (Schedules 2 and 3 of the Bank Act).

An analysis shows (Figs. 6.1 and 6.2) that, while local banks, which are the largest in terms of total assets, are retail-focused and diversified retail institutions, credit unions are overwhelmingly retail-focused and foreign banks, which are the smallest across all three business models.

Appendix C provides descriptive statistics for these banks and credit unions for the overall period of analysis.

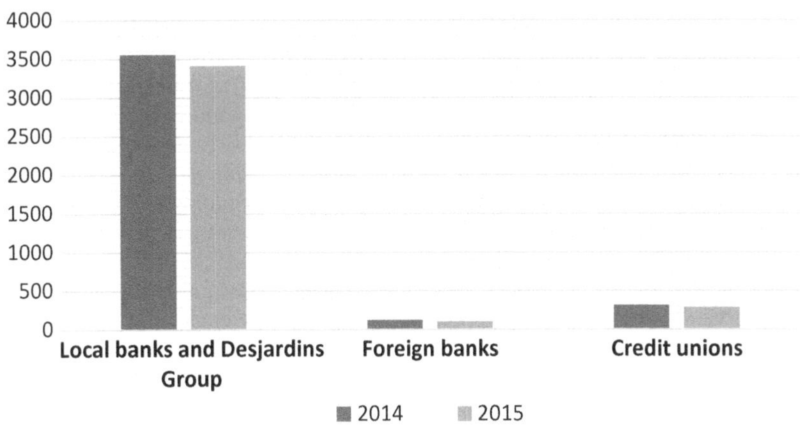

Fig. 6.1 Total size of institution type, 2010–2015 (billions in Canadian dollars). Source: Author

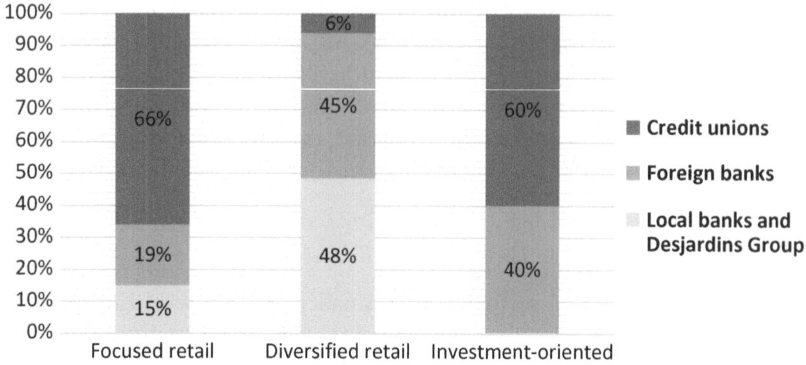

Fig. 6.2 Distribution of type of institution across business models (2010–2015, % of assets). Source: Author

To conclude, crossing business models in banks with size and ownership and organisational structures show that business models analysis adds a new analytical dimension to better understand the architecture of the banking system and to contribute to financial stability assessment and stability.

References

Ayadi, R., D.T. Llewelyn, R.H. Schmidt, E. Arbak and W.P. de Groen (2010), *Investigating Diversity in the Banking Sector in Europe: Key Developments, Performance and Role of Cooperative Banks*, Centre for European Policy Studies (CEPS), Brussels (https://www.ceps.eu/publications/investigating-diversity-banking-sector-europe-key-developments-performance-and-role).

Ayadi, R., R.H. Schmidt, S. Carbo Valverde, E. Arbak and F. Rodriguez Fernandez (2009), *Investigating Diversity in the Banking Sector in Europe: The Performance and Role of Savings Banks*, Centre for European Policy Studies (CEPS), Brussels (https://www.ceps.eu/publications/investigating-diversity-banking-sector-europe-performance-and-role-savings-banks).

Ayadi, R. and G. Pujals (2005), "Banking mergers and acquisitions in the EU: Overview, assessment and prospects", June, SUERF, Vienna.

Ayadi, R. et al. (2016), "Banking Business Models Monitor 2015: Europe", Montreal, International Research Centre On Cooperative Finance, HEC Montreal.

Ayadi, R. et al. (2017), "Bank and Credit Unions Business Models in the United States", Montreal, International Research Centre On Cooperative Finance, HEC Montreal.

CHAPTER 7

Migration of Business Models

Changing business models, hereafter called "**migration**",[1] can provide a wealth of information to market participants, regulators, creditors and depositors about the strategy of banks and their behaviour in the markets where they are active in and about their risk profiles and their contribution to **systemic risk** over time.

This chapter explains the reasons why banks change their business models and describes the migration process of business models in banks in Europe, US and Canada.

7.1 Migration of Business Models

Banks are not expected to change their business models frequently; however, transformations occur in a changing environment and institutions are expected to adapt their business models for the following reasons:

1. to respond to market forces, competitive pressures (i.e. competition and race to profits, mergers and acquisitions, overall sector's restructuring movement) and financial and economic crises;
2. to respond to regulatory, monetary, structural reforms and other government led decisions (i.e. increase of capital, liquidity and resolution

[1] Term used in Ayadi et al. (2016, 2017) to describe the process of changing business models in banks.

R. Ayadi, *Banking Business Models*, Palgrave Macmillan Studies in Banking and Financial Institutions,
https://doi.org/10.1007/978-3-030-02248-8_7

requirements, changes in monetary policy, state aid decisions with a restructuring plan requirement);
3. to adapt to technological transformations and financial innovations (e.g. fintech, artificial intelligence and big data, blockchain and virtual currencies);
4. to adapt to the macro-economic cycle (e.g. real estate booms and busts, governments, corporates and consumers indebtedness)
5. other reasons (i.e. major banks failures, political events (e.g. exit of UK from the EU) or major scandals.)

All these reasons could be essential to understand banks' behaviours and their consequences on systemic risk and financial stability.

Although the composition of banks under the different business models is expected to remain relatively steady over time, transitions do occur and more so in some models than in others.

Migration from one business model to another can be assessed looking at:

1. the number of institutions (or observations); and the total assets of institutions that migrated every year and during the period for one country and for the region (e.g. EU, EEA or Eurozone);
2. the direction to which banks migrate (e.g. from retail to investment or within different types of retail business models);
3. the determinants of migration; and
4. the frequency of migrations

Understanding the migration process of business models in banks is essential for understanding the process of accumulation or dissipation of systemic risk. It serves as a monitoring tool for a frequent financial stability assessment at a country, regional and global levels. The consequences on financial stability are different when banks change their business models to less risky activities and more stable funding profiles or to more risky and short-term activities and less stable and volatile funding profiles. The transformational process includes banks of different business models, which mix and evolution would lead to either to more or less risky business models and hence to more or less risky financial system.

In what follows we provide the assessment of migration of business models in banks in Europe, in banks and credit unions in the US and in banks and credit unions in Canada.

7.2 Migration of Business Models in Banks in Europe

Looking at data from 2005 to 2014, Ayadi et al. (2016) provided the business models transition matrix for banks in Europe, which shows that business models do not behave similarly.

Figure 7.1 provides the transition matrix for the five models from 2005 to 2014.

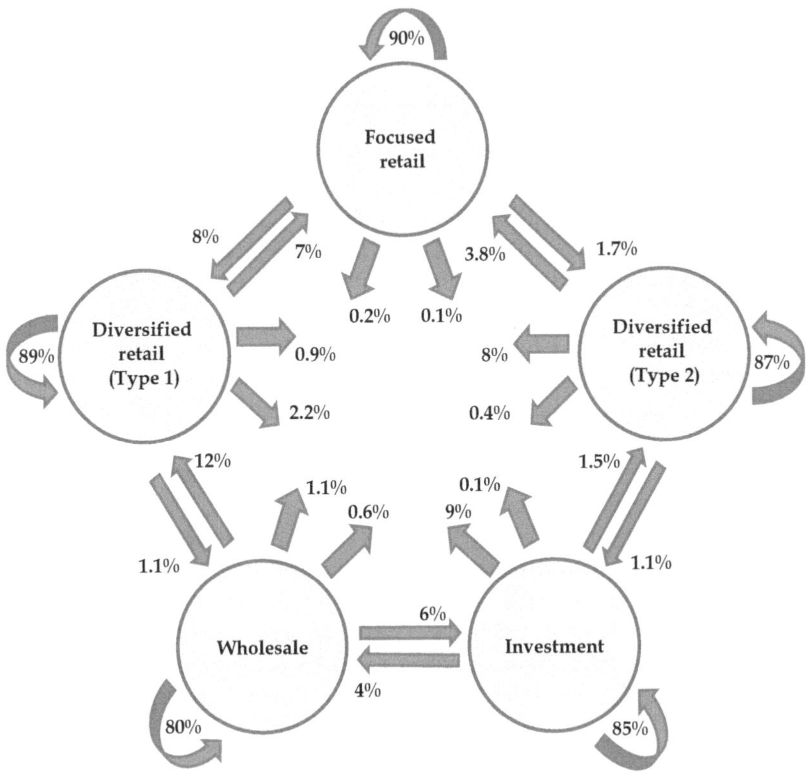

Fig. 7.1 Model transition matrix, share of banks in Europe (%, 2005–2014). Source: Reproduced from Ayadi et al. (2016). Note: The figures give the share of banks that belong to a specific model in one period switching to another model (or remaining assigned to the same model) in the next period

The focused retail model shows the highest persistence; 90% of the banks remained the same from one year to the next, followed by the diversified retail, wholesale and investment banks which remained within the same model throughout the sampled years (89%, 87%, 80% and 85% respectively).

Seven per cent of diversified retail (type 1) banks and 3.8% diversified retail (type 2) migrated to focused retail. Of wholesale banks, 5.9% migrated to investment banks and 4.0% from investment banks moved to wholesale banks.

The net effect of these migrations is not straightforward and further research is needed to assess this effect over time.

7.3 Migration of Business Models in the US

Looking more closely at the migrations between bank business models in the US, Fig. 7.2 provides the transition matrix for the four models from 2000 to 2014. Roughly, 80% of the population of each business model has kept their activity-funding pattern over the decade and half under study: the incidence of migrations among business models ranges from 11% to 20%.

The assignment of banks to the focused retail (type 2) model shows the highest persistence; 88.8% of the banks remained the same from one year to the next. The vast majority of the retail (type 1), wholesale-oriented and investment-oriented banks remained within the same model throughout the sampled years (79.9%, 79.8% and 83.4% respectively). The notable migrations were primarily to retail (type 1), with flows of 15.7% from investment-oriented, 10.9% from retail (type 2) and 5.4% from wholesale-oriented banks. The other large migration flows are to retail (type 2) banks, with 14.1% migrating from retail (type 1) and 11.5% of wholesale-oriented banks. Many wholesale-oriented banks further migrated to investment-oriented banks (5.4%) and an almost similar proportion (5.9%) of retail (type 1) banks migrated to investment-oriented banks.

For the credit unions in the US, although the composition of the different models remains relatively steady over time, transitions do occur—and more in some models than in others. Figure 7.3 provides the transition matrix for the three models over the period from 2000 to 2014. The assignment of credit unions to the retail type 3 and retail type 1 model

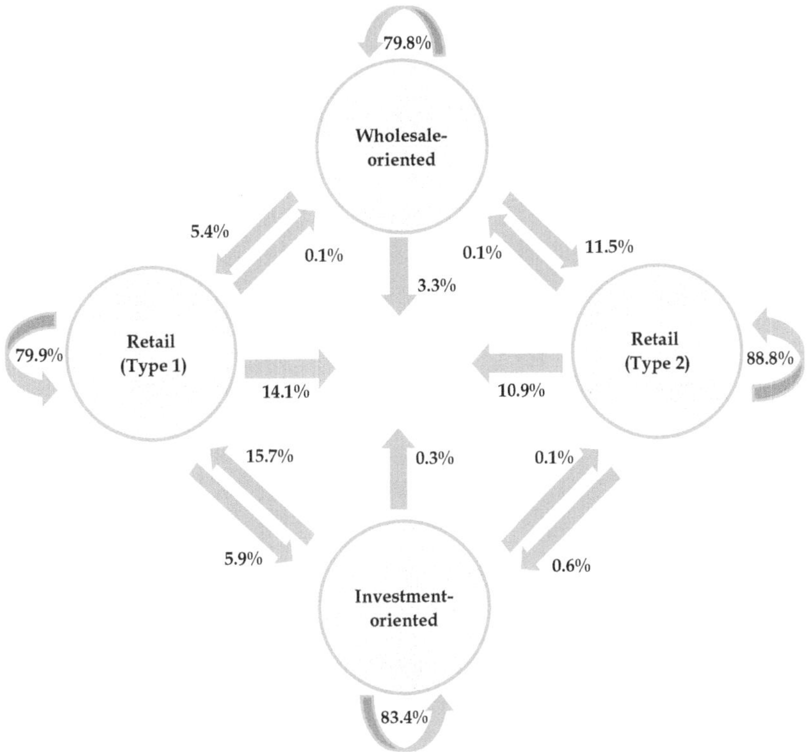

Fig. 7.2 Model transition matrix, share of banks in the US (2000–2014). Source: Reproduced from Ayadi et al. (2017). Note: The amounts in percentages give the share of banks that belong to a specific model in one period switching to another model (or remaining assigned to the same model) in the next period

shows the highest persistence; 83.7% and 82.5% respectively of the credit unions of these groups remained the same from one year to the next. The retail type 2 credit unions showed a lower persistence with only 74.4% of the institutions remaining within the same model. The migration was primarily between retail type 1 and retail type 2 and retail type 2 and retail type 3, with flows ranging between 12.0% and 16.9%. The migration between retail type 1 and retail type 3 was substantially less with just 0.6% and 0.9% to and from retail type 3.

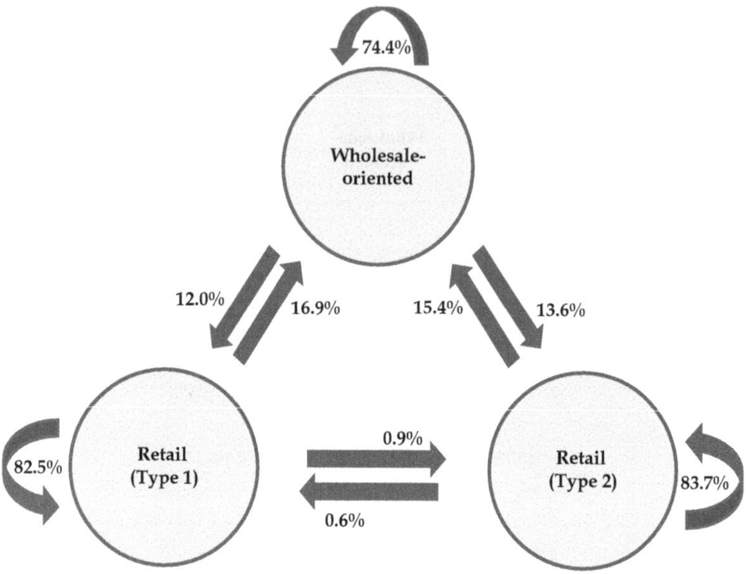

Fig. 7.3 Model transition matrix, share of credit unions in the US (2000–2014). Source: Reproduced from Ayadi et al. (2017). Note: The figures give the share of credit unions that belong to a specific model in one period switching to another model (or remaining assigned to the same model) in the next period

7.4 Migration of Business Models in Canada

Looking more closely at the migrations between bank and credit business models in Canada, Fig. 7.4 provides the transition matrix for the four models from 2010 to 2015.

More than 90% of the population of each business model has kept their activity-funding pattern over the decade and half under study: the incidence of migrations among business models is very low. Investment banks have not changed their business models over the period. The retail focused also shows a high level of business model stability (97.5%). Banks under the retail diversified business model migrate to either focused retail (5.2%) or to investment (2.6%).

As compared to Europe and US business models, Canadian bank and credit unions business models are relatively more stable.

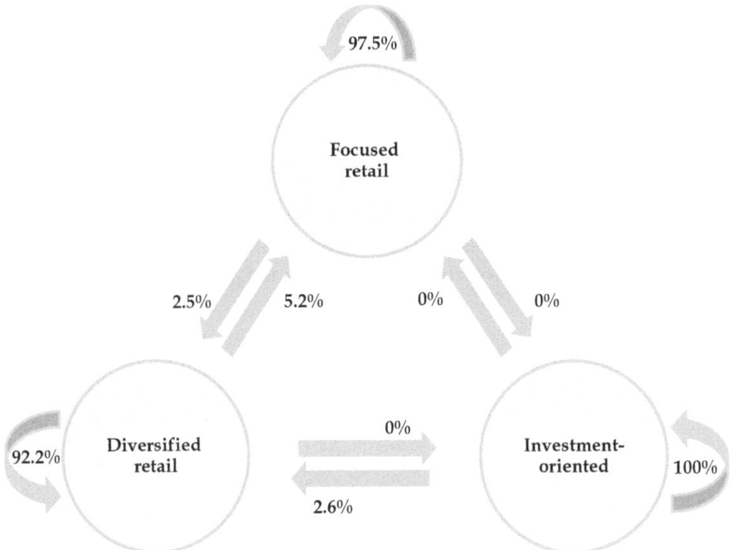

Fig. 7.4 Model transition matrix, share of banks in Canada (%, 2010–2015). Source: Author. Note: The figures give the share of banks that belong to a specific model in one period switching to another model (or remaining assigned to the same model) in the next period

To conclude, the migration analysis shows a generally low percentage of business models migration between business models. This migration of business models of banks and credit unions is a phenomenon that has been recently researched in the literature.[2] More research on the determinants and consequences of business models migration is needed to examine this process particularly in terms of financial stability and instability assessment and management. Moreover, when comparing the three banking systems in Europe, US and Canada, the lower percentage of migrating banks in Canada, among other factors (size, regulation), can explain the stability of the banking system pre- and post-financial crisis. The percentage of migrating business models can become an additional indicator for financial stability and instability assessment and management.

[2] Ayadi et al. (2018) show that, in Europe, bank business model stability increases the overall bank soundness, whilst banks switching their business model are closer to default.

References

Ayadi, R. et al. (2016), "Banking Business Models Monitor 2015: Europe", Montreal, International Research Centre On Cooperative Finance, HEC Montreal.

Ayadi, R. et al. (2017), "Bank and Credit Unions Business Models in the United States", Montreal, International Research Centre On Cooperative Finance, HEC Montreal.

Ayadi, R., Ferri, G. and V. Pesic (2018), "Does business model instability imperil banks' soundness: Evidence from Europe" Bancaria, No. 7–8, July–August, Italy.

CHAPTER 8

Performance of Business Models

Banks and other financial institutions must be economically and financially viable. To assess their financial and **economic performance**, several indicators are used. If a bank is not performing as compared to its peers, then it will not honour its financial obligations with its clients, depositors and creditors. Therefore, performance is a key indicator that must be monitored frequently as part of the financial stability assessment framework.

This chapter discusses the financial and economic performance metrics and shows the results of business models performance for banks and credit unions in Europe, US and Canada.

8.1 Performance Indicators

A large variety of financial performance indicators are used to assess the performance of business models of banks and credit unions in Europe, US and Canada. These indicators range from profitability, efficiency, income distribution and contribution to the real economy. The descriptive statistics are in Appendix D.

The two key profitability indicators that are widely used in the banking literature to assess financial performance of banks and other financial institutions are as follows:

R. Ayadi, *Banking Business Models*, Palgrave Macmillan Studies in Banking and Financial Institutions,
https://doi.org/10.1007/978-3-030-02248-8_8

1. **Return on assets (ROA):** Income before taxes[1]/Total assets; and
2. **Return on equity (ROE):** Income before taxes/Total equity.

The higher the ROA and ROE, the more profitable the banks are.

For credit unions total equity is replaced by net worth. The net worth signals the capital strength of a credit union as it also includes retained earnings.

Other additional economic performance indicators are used to assess:

Cost efficiency shows how efficient a bank is in terms of its cost to income:

1. **Cost-to-income ratio (CIR)**: operational expenses/income from operations.
   This indicator measures efficiency

Since it is a cost, a higher CIR indicates that an institution is less efficient. A lower indicator shows that an institution is more efficient.

For credit unions, the denominator is total gross income.

Income distribution is important as an alternative indication of how a bank captures income from the risks it takes.

2. **Net interest income**: Total interest income/Total interest expense
   This indicator measures the extent of intermediation activity.
3. **Commission and fees**: Income from fiduciary activities, service charges on deposit accounts in government offices, trading gains from foreign exchange transactions, other foreign transaction gains, gains and fees from assets held in trading accounts and other non-interest income.
4. **Trading income**: Net gain realised during the calendar year-to-date from the sale, exchange, redemption or retirement of all securities reported as held-to-maturity securities and available-for-sale securities. This indicator only applies to banks.

[1]The two profitability indicators are computed with data on pre-tax income to ensure comparability across the many US tax jurisdictions, European countries and Canada, and with credit unions.

Contribution to the real economy indicates how much the banks finance the real economy:

5. **Customer loan growth**: (Gross customer loan of the current year/ Gross customer loans of previous year)/Gross customer loan of the previous year.

8.2 Performance of Business Models in Europe

According to the empirical investigation in Ayadi et al. (2016) reported in Table 8.1, the diversified retail (type 1) banks reported both the highest return on assets and return on equity of all the business models. The median values are, however, significantly higher than those of the other retail-oriented models. In turn, the diversified retail (type 2) banks reported significantly lower returns.

The results for ownership structures show that the median return on assets is significantly higher for commercial banks, while the nationalised banks report the lowest. The results for return on equity are relatively closer to one another, with the cooperative banks reporting the highest values.

The median efficiency scores for all the business models are relatively close to the median for all banks, with the diversified retail banks (type 2) reporting the lowest cost-to-income ratios and the wholesale banks the highest. The differences across ownership structures are larger, with the public banks appearing most efficient and the commercial and cooperative banks least efficient.

The breakdown of the income confirms that retail-oriented banks have high amounts of interest income and investment banks have higher amount of trading income. The breakdown of income into its components can also be used as a good proxy for business models of banks.

In terms of median values for customer loan growth, the retail-focused banks reported the highest loan growth. The loan growth is significantly higher than that of all other business models, except for wholesale banks. The diversified retail (type 2) banks reported the significantly lower loan growth. The differences between the ownership structures are, nevertheless, larger. The public banks reported the highest loan growth, while the nationalised banks were the only banks reporting negative loan growth.

Table 8.1 Profitability, efficiency, income distribution and contribution to real economy indicators in Europe

(a) Business models

	Model 1—Focused retail (%)	*Model 2—Diversified retail (type 1) (%)*	*Model 3—Diversified retail (type 2) (%)*	*Model 4—Wholesale (%)*	*Model 5—Investment (%)*	*All (%)*
Return on assets (RoA)	0.47**	0.50**	0.40****	0.49*	0.46*	0.48
Return on equity (RoE)	7.64***	8.09***	5.39***	6.15***	8.04**	7.60
Cost-to-income ratio (CIR)	64.5****	66.7**	61.9****	69.8**	68.0**	65.6
Net interest	75.1****	73.6****	65.4****	40.7****	54.0****	72.3
Commission & fees	18.4****	20.6****	19.7****	38.4****	21.9****	20.2
Trading	1.4****	0.0****	4.0**	3.8**	4.4**	0.4
Other	3.0****	3.8***	6.9****	2.2****	3.5***	3.8
Customer loan growth	4.64***	3.42**	1.11****	4.47*	2.95**	3.61

(b) Ownership structures

	Commercial (%)	*Cooperative (%)*	*Nationalised (%)*	*Public (%)*	*Savings (%)*	*All (%)*
Return on assets (RoA)	0.62****	0.47***	0.14****	0.49**	0.45***	0.48
Return on equity (RoE)	7.07**	7.97****	3.98****	6.75***	7.53***	7.59
Cost-to-income ratio (CIR)	66.8***	66.4***	60.0****	56.9****	64.5****	65.6
Net interest	58.9****	73.6***	66.9****	73.1**	74.7***	72.3
Commission & fees	23.9****	19.8**	18.3*	17.3***	19.6**	20.2
Trading	5.1**	0.0****	5.0**	5.3**	0.1****	0.4
Other	3.1***	4.0**	3.9*	1.9****	4.1**	3.8
Customer loan growth	4.51**	3.83***	−2.69****	5.78***	2.87****	3.62

Source: Reproduced from Ayadi et al. (2016)

Notes: All figures are the median values for the year-end observations for the relevant sub-sample. The independence of clusters was tested using non-parametric equality-of-medians two-sample tests at 5% significance. According to the results of these tests, the number of asterisks (*, **, *** or ****) stands for the statistical difference of any given cluster from that of other clusters for that indicator. For example, three asterisks (***) imply that the cluster or ownership structure is statistically different from the three (furthest) clusters/ownership structure but not the fourth (closest) one

8.3 Performance of Business Models in the US

According to the empirical investigation in Ayadi et al. (2017) reported in Table 8.2, a comparative performance assessment is provided across business models and bank size categories.

Retail type 1 banks reported both the highest return on assets and return on equity of all the bank business models. More precisely, ROAs for the two retail business models are the highest, almost equal, and statistically distinct from those for the other business models.

Wholesale-oriented banks posted the lowest ROA but the second-highest ROE of all the bank business models, but the latter ranking could not be confirmed statistically. ROAs for the other business models are all close to the sample mean, whereas ROEs are more distinct.

Across bank size categories, the mid-sized banks dominate their peers both with respect to ROA and ROE. Similarly, micro banks were the least active according to both return measures. In between, the results for the very small and large banks, for both ROA and ROE, are relatively close to one another. Among credit unions, retail type 1 institutions have the highest ROE, followed by retail type 2 and retail type 3. The ROAs of retail type 1 and retail type 2 banks are the two highest and are not statistically different.

Wholesale-oriented and investment-oriented banks are the least efficient business models, reporting significantly higher cost-to-income ratios. The two retail business models are the most efficient. The mean efficiency scores for all the other business models are relatively close to the mean for all banks. The differences across size categories are equally large, with the micro banks appearing to be the least efficient and the small and mid-sized banks operating significantly more efficiently. Large banks operate at an efficiency level close to the sample average. The differences between the credit union business models are significant. With the highest efficiency scores, the retail type 3 credit unions are by far the least efficient and the retail type 1 the most efficient.

In terms of growth of customer loans, the retail (type 2) banks reported the highest loan growth, followed by the retail type 1 banks. Their respective loan growth is significantly higher than those of all other business models. The wholesale-oriented banks reported the lowest, negative loan growth, which is not significantly different from the loan growth of investment-oriented banks, also negative. The differences between sizes of

Table 8.2 Performance, income distribution and contribution to real economy indicators in the US

(a) Bank business models

	Model 1—Wholesale oriented (%)	*Model 2—Retail (type 1) (%)*	*Model 3—Retail (type 2) (%)*	*Model 4—Investment oriented (%)*	*All (%)*
Return on assets (ROA)	1.15**	1.35**	1.35**	1.2**	1.28
Return on equity (ROE)	12.40	12.5**	12.05*	12.07*	12.31
Cost-to-income ratio (CIR)	63.28**	61.04***	59.53***	62.54**	61.26
Net interest (as % of total income)	48.83***	62.79***	67.31***	60.61***	60.39
Commission & fees (as % of total income)	34.33***	21.61***	18.35***	23.65***	24.07
Trading (as % of total income)	0.34*	0.57**	0.19**	0.74***	0.40
Customer loan growth	−0.38**	2.81***	8.93***	−0.13**	4.42

(b) Bank size categories

	Micro (<$1 bn) (%)	*Very small (1–$5 bn) (%)*	*Small (5–$10 bn) (%)*	*Mid ($10–$50 bn) (%)*	*Large (>$50 bn) (%)*	*All (%)*
Return on assets (ROA)	1.1***	1.32**	1.5**	1.75***	1.21**	1.28
Return on equity (ROE)	10.36****	12.01**	13.29**	15.94****	11.91**	12.31
Cost-to-income ratio (CIR)	68.58****	62.44***	57.89***	56.24***	61.17***	61.26
Net interest	74.8****	67.54***	67.42***	58.73***	56.87***	60.39
Commission & fees	17.03****	21.38***	19.63***	23.66***	26.03***	24.07
Trading	0.34	0.18	−0.20	0.28	0.51	0.40
Customer loan growth	4.38**	3.81**	12.32****	9.03****	3.62**	4.42

(c) Credit union business models

	Retail type 1 (%)	*Retail type 2 (%)*	*Retail type 3 (%)*	*All (%)*
Return on assets (ROA)	0.7*	0.68*	0.4**	0.68
Return on equity (ROE)	6.54**	5.8**	2.78**	6.02
Cost-to-income ratio (CIR)	73.1**	74.22**	81.84**	73.80
Net interest	52.78**	55.94**	61.51**	54.15
Commission & fees	13.89**	13.48**	11.62**	13.67
Trading	0.02**	0*	0*	0.00
Customer loan growth	7.89**	4.03**	1.45**	6.48

Source: Reproduced from Ayadi et al. (2017)

Notes: All figures are weighted averages for the year-end observations for the business models/size categories. The independence of clusters was tested using Welch two-sample tests at 5% significance. To report the results of these tests, the number of asterisks (*, **, *** or ****) stands for the statistical difference of any given business model/size category from that of other business models/size categories for that indicator. For example, two asterisks (**) in sub-table b imply that the size category is statistically different from the two (furthest) size categories but not the third and fourth (closest) ones category are similarly pronounced, with micro, very small and large banks reporting an overall loan growth significantly higher than those of mid-sized and small banks. These latter size categories reported the highest loan growth over the period. Among the credit union business models, there is a significantly large difference in the weighted average loan growth. While the retail type 1 credit unions reported substantial increases in their customer loans, the loan book of the retail type 2 credit unions has moderately expanded and the increase in loans provided by retail type 3 credit unions is rather weak.

8.4 Performance of Business Models in Canada

As reported in Table 8.3, the diversified retail banks reported both the highest return on assets and return on equity of all the business models. All types of banks reported high performance.

The breakdown of the income confirms that the focused retail-oriented banks have high amounts of interest income and the investment banks have higher amount of trading income.

In terms of customer loan growth, the retail diversified banks reported the highest loan growth. The majority of these banks are domestic.

When assessing the performance of business models of banks and credit unions over the periods of analysis, the results show that profitability, efficiency, income breakdown and contribution to the real economy differ by business model, ownership structure and size of banks and credit unions in Europe, the US and Canada. Banks in the US and Canada are generally more profitable than banks in Europe, while except for the credit unions in the US, the efficiency scores are close to their average values. Generally, retail-oriented banks drive the contribution to the real economy, while investment banks are more oriented towards trading and commission-generating activities.

Monitoring the evolution of profitability, efficiency, income distribution and contribution to the real economy per business model, size and ownership structure is important to assess the capacity of the financial system to contribute to the real economy. The performance metrics used should also be considered in the financial stability assessment.

Table 8.3 Performance, income and contribution to real economy indicators in Canada

(a) Business models

	Model 1—Diversified retail (%)	*Model 2—Focused retail (%)*	*Model 3—Investment oriented (%)*	*All (%)*
Return on assets (RoA)	1.04**	0.75**	0.54**	1.02
Return on equity (RoE)	17.94**	11.32**	5.49**	17.50
Cost-to-income ratio (CIR)	62.96*	68.56*	67.00	63.15
Net interest	49.59**	78.21**	23.8**	50.39
Commission & fees	23.97*	15.67**	25.39*	23.63
Trading	5.97**	1.46**	17.53**	5.88
Customer loan growth	5.14	2.25	−13.72	4.92

(b) Institution type

	Local banks and Desjardins group (%)	*Foreign banks (%)*	*Credit unions (%)*	*All (%)*
Return on assets (RoA)	1.04	1.07	0.60	1.02
Return on equity (RoE)	18.06	11.97	9.40	17.50
Cost-to-income ratio (CIR)	63.10	54.43	74.67	63.15
Net interest	49.72	54.84	72.15	50.39
Commission & fees	23.75	30.56	17.87	23.63
Trading	5.87	9.12	2.63	5.88
Customer loan growth	5.42	−3.88	0.92	4.93

Source: Author

Notes: All figures are the weighted averages values for the year-end observations for the relevant sub-sample. The independence of clusters was tested using non-parametric equality-of-weighted averages two-sample tests at 5% significance. According to the results of these tests, the number of asterisks (*, **, *** or ****) stands for the statistical difference of any given cluster from that of other clusters for that indicator. For example, three asterisks (***) imply that the cluster or ownership structure is statistically different from the three (furthest) business models/ownership structure but not the fourth (closest) one

References

Ayadi, R. et al. (2016), "Banking Business Models Monitor 2015: Europe", Montreal, International Research Centre On Cooperative Finance, HEC Montreal.

Ayadi, R. et al. (2017), "Bank and Credit Unions Business Models in the United States", Montreal, International Research Centre On Cooperative Finance, HEC Montreal.

CHAPTER 9

Risk of Business Models

Banks and other financial institutions take and manage different types of risks in the financial system. These risks range from credit risk, market risk, operational risk to counterparty risk and reputational risk, to name a few. Depending on their business model, ownership structure and size, banks and other financial institutions can take excessive unmanaged risk; when accumulated in the system, this risk may cause disruptions that are detrimental to the stability and safety of the financial system.

This chapter exposes the risks indicators used and shows the results of business models risks for banks and credit unions in Europe, US and Canada.

9.1 Risk Indicators

Several risks indicators are useful to assess the risks of business models of banks and credit unions in Europe, US and Canada. The following balance sheet (i.e. Z-score, loan loss provision and size of government exposures) and market indicators which are only available for listed financial institutions (i.e. average daily stock returns, annual standard deviations in daily stock returns and Credit Derivatives Swaps (CDS) spread for senior and subordinated bonds) are used and tested:

Z-score or distance to default: The **Z-score** is a balance sheet-based indicator that provides an estimate of a bank's distance to default. In essence, the risk measure uses historical earnings volatility and returns,

R. Ayadi, *Banking Business Models*, Palgrave Macmillan Studies in Banking and Financial Institutions,
https://doi.org/10.1007/978-3-030-02248-8_9

as well as current capital levels, to construct the level of a (one-time) shock beyond the historical average that would lead to default.

The greater the Z-score, the further a bank is from default and the lower is the probability of a default.[1]

This indicator has also been constructed for credit unions in the US, with current capital levels proxied by the net worth.

Loan loss provisions: It is the value needed to make the allowance for loan and lease losses adequate to absorb expected loan and lease losses, based upon management's evaluation of the reporting institution's current loan and lease portfolio and value of the provision for allocated transfer risk, if the institution is required to maintain an allocated transfer reserve by the International Lending Supervision Act of 1983 in the case of the US.

The size (and concentration) of the government exposure in banks' balance sheet: This indicator shows the sovereign exposures in banks' balance sheets. According to the Basel rules, banks do not have to hold any capital against most of the OECD (Organisation for Economic Co-operation and Development) countries government exposures and there is no restriction on the exposures. However, the write-down on the Greek government bonds through the Private Sector Involvement (PSI) in early 2012 showed, however, that Euro area sovereign debt is not actually risk-free and these governments can fail in paying their obligations. The higher the size of government exposure (and concentration to the home country "home bias"), the riskier the business model of the bank is.

Average daily stock returns: This indicator only applies to banks and holding companies and not to credit unions and other institutions that are not listed.

Generally, only part of the assets of the banks are accounted at fair value, while the equity markets are considered to value the entire bank according to market principles. The changing economic circumstances are, therefore, considered to impact on the market values faster than the book values particularly for the listed banks.

Annual standard deviations in daily stock returns have been calculated by annualising the standard deviation of daily stock returns and. This indicator only applies to listed banks (not to credit unions) and measures the risk sensitivity of these institutions.

[1] For full details on the computation, see Appendix F.

Credit Derivatives Swaps spread for senior and subordinated bonds: The CDS spread is a market indicator for credit risk used by market participants to assess and hedge the credit risks for senior and subordinated exposures. The CDS spread is the premium that the buyer of the protection pays to the seller of the protection. The higher the CDS spread, the higher the risk. The data on the CDS spreads is collected from Markit database.

Descriptive statistics are in Appendix D.

9.2 Risk of Business Models in Europe

The empirical investigation to assess risks of business models of banks in Europe in Ayadi et al. (2016) is reported in Table 9.1 and Appendix F.

The deposit-funded-focused retail and diversified retail (type 1) banks have the greatest distance to default (i.e. less exposed to default), whereas the more market-funded-diversified retail (type 2), wholesale and investment banks are closer to default. The markets perceive the default probabilities for the focused retail and diversified retail (type 1) to be higher than for the other business models. This is confirmed by the median values of the loan losses for diversified retail (type 1) banks that are also distinct from the other models. The default risks might be further aggravated by the high concentration in government exposures.

The results across ownership structures are more straightforward. The stakeholder-value banks are farthest away from default, whereas the shareholder value banks are closest to default. In particular, the nationalised banks are risky, with the highest loan loss provisions, highest stock return volatility, highest credit default swap-rates (CDS) and large domestically concentrated government exposures. However, the latter feature is not statistically a distinguishing one across ownership structures. The commercial banks are doing considerably better on the different risk indicators and are within the range of the cooperative and savings banks. The public banks seem to benefit from the close ties with government. The loan loss provisions are close to zero and the CDS rates are the lowest among all ownership structures.

9.3 Risk of Business Models in the US

The empirical investigation in Ayadi et al. (2017) for the US is reported in Table 9.2 and Appendix D. The results across bank business models show that, overall, the weighted average Z-score is surprisingly low (just over 20).

Table 9.1 Risk indicators in Europe

(a) Business models

	Focused retail	*Diversified retail (type 1)*	*Diversified retail (type 2)*	*Wholesale*	*Investment*	*All*
Z-score (std dev. from default)	52.8****	59.8****	20.5****	26.6****	22.9****	43.7
Loan loss provisions (% of gross customer loans)	0.29%***	0.84%****	0.56%***	0.29%**	0.44%**	0.43%
Stock returns (avg. daily returns)	0.012%*	0.027%	0.035%**	–0.047%*	0.027%	0.021%
Stock returns volatility (std dev. of daily returns)	1.9%*	2.2%**	2.0%	1.9%	2.0%*	2.0%
CDS spread (senior, annual avg.)	1.9%***	2.0%***	1.0%**	0.8%**	1.0%**	1.2%
CDS spread (subordinated, annual avg.)	3.7%***	2.8%***	1.6%**	0.2%**	1.6%**	1.8%
Government exposure (% of own funds)	117%	190.3%	187.6%	21.3%	152.2%	165.8%
Home country exposure (% of government exp.)	98%	86.8%	80.7%	51%	49.3%	84.7%

(b) Ownership structures

	Commercial	*Cooperative*	*Nationalised*	*Public*	*Savings*	*All*
Z-score (std dev. from default)	18.1****	64.7****	2.5****	34.0****	54.7****	43.2
Loan loss provisions (% of gross customer loans)	0.49%***	0.54%**	0.77%***	0.05%****	0.26%****	0.43%
Stock returns (avg. daily returns)	0.022%	−0.022%	0.032%	0.012%	0.031%	0.022%
Stock returns volatility (std dev. of daily returns)	2.1%****	2.7%****	3.8%****	0.9%****	1.9%****	2.0%
CDS spread (senior, annual avg.)	1.1%**	1.2%**	1.7%****	0.4%****	1.3%**	1.2%
CDS spread (subordinated, annual avg.)	1.6%	1.8%	2.5%	–	2.0%	1.8%
Government exposure (% of own funds)	137.5%	154.8%	222.9%	311.1%	190%	163.9%
Home country exposure (% of government exp.)	67.7%	84.8%	85.5%	84.8%	90.2%	84.7%

Source: Reproduced from Ayadi et al. (2016)

Notes: All figures are the median values for the relevant sub-sample. The independence of clusters and ownership structures was tested using non-parametric equality-of-medians two-sample tests at 5% significance. According to the results of these tests, the number of asterisks (*, **, *** or ****) stands for the statistical difference of any given cluster/ownership structure from that number of other clusters/ownership structures for that indicator. For example, two asterisks (**) imply that the cluster is statistically different from two (furthest) clusters but not the third (closest) one. See Appendix G for the assumptions pertaining to the construction of the net stable funding ratio (NSFR) measure

Table 9.2 Risk Indicators in the US

(a) Bank business models

	Model 1—Wholesale oriented	*Model 2—Retail (type 1)*	*Model 3—Retail (type 2)*	*Model 4—Investment oriented*	*All*
Z-score (std dev. from default)	18.29**	21.58***	18.64**	22.99***	20.04
Loan loss provisions (% of gross customer loans)	1.7%***	0.85%***	1.08%***	0.46%***	1.07%
Stock returns (avg. daily returns)	0.44%	0.33%	0.35%	0.25%	0.34%
Stock returns (std dev. of daily returns)	3.9%**	4.3%**	5.4%***	3.5%*	4.8%

(b) Bank size categories

	Micro (<1 bn)	*Very small (1–5 bn)*	*Small (5–10 bn)*	*Mid (10–50 bn)*	*Large (>50 bn)*	*All*
Z-score (std dev. from default)	24.51****	21.65***	21.08**	16.97****	19.59***	20.04
Loan loss provisions (% of gross customer loans)	0.6%****	0.89%***	0.9%***	1.19%***	1.18%***	1.07%
Stock returns (avg. daily returns)	0.46%****	0.08%*	0.05%*	0.04%*	0.04%*	0.34%
Stock returns (std dev. daily returns)	5.9%****	2.8%****	2.2%**	2.0%**	2.4%**	4.8%

(c) Credit union business models

	Retail type 1	*Retail type 2*	*Retail type 3*	*All*
Z-score (std dev. from default)	29.02**	31.60**	30.08**	30.04
Loan loss provisions (% of gross customer loans)	0.74%**	0.58%**	0.53%**	0.68%

Source: Reproduced from Ayadi et al. (2017)

Notes: The Z-score and loan loss provision figures are weighted averages for the year-end observations for the business models/bank size categories. The independence of business models or bank size categories was tested using Welch two-sample tests at 5% significance. Stock returns and their standard deviations are median values for the year-end observations for the business models/bank size categories. The independence of clusters was tested using non-parametric Wilcoxon-Mann-Witney two-sample tests at 5% significance. To report the results of these tests, the number of asterisks (*, **, *** or ****) stands for the statistical difference of any given business model/bank size category from that number of other business models/bank size categories for that indicator. For example, two asterisks (**) in sub-table imply that the business model is statistically different from the two (furthest) business models but not the third (closest) one

Within this average, the distance to default for the entire period was largest for investment-oriented banks, followed by retail (type 1). The wholesale-oriented and retail (type 2) banks are the closest to default. Loan loss provisions show a different picture, with the weighted average loan loss provisions of wholesale-oriented banks significantly above and those of investment-oriented banks below those of both types of retail banks. The retail (type 2) banks that are closer to default have the second largest loan loss provisions.

Stock returns are largest for wholesale banks, but the ranking is not statistically significant. The riskiness of banks measured by the standard deviation of stock returns indicates that investment banks are the least risky. Results are, however, only significantly different from those for retail (type 2) banks that have the highest standard deviations. The difference between wholesale and both retail banks is also significant.

Turning to the results across bank size categories, within an average low Z-score for the overall industry, micro banks were furthest from default, while mid-sized banks are closest to default. The Z-score of very small, small and large banks were statistically indifferent from each other. Loan loss provisions almost follow bank sizes, that is, the larger the size category, the higher the weighted average loan loss provisions as a share of total gross customer loans. At the lower end of the size range, micro banks have posted provision levels that are statistically distinctive from the other business models.

The stock returns are also not significantly different across bank size categories, except for the stock returns of the micro banks, which were significantly higher than for all the other size categories. The differences in volatility are, in most cases, significant. The standard deviation of the daily returns of micro banks and very small banks are significantly higher than for all the other sizes of bank. Hence, these might thus be considered by investors to be more risky.

The results across credit union business models show that retail type 1 credit unions were closest to default, although the differences with retail type 2 and retail type 3, albeit statistically significant, are not pronounced. In turn, retail type 1 credit unions posted the highest provisions for loan losses, while retail type 3 credit unions, which are furthest from default, have the lowest loan loss provisions. The weighted average values for both the Z-score and loan loss provisions are significantly different across all credit union business models.

9.4 Risk of Business Models in Canada

The results across bank business models in Table 9.3 and Appendix D show that, overall, the weighted average Z-score is quite high reaching 126. Within this average, the distance to default for the entire period was

Table 9.3 Risk indicators in Canada

(a) Business models

	Model 1—Diversified retail	*Model 2—Focused retail*	*Model 3—Investment oriented*	*All*
Z-score (std dev. from default)	130.1442**	56.6112*	53.4612*	126.7421
Loan loss provisions (% of gross customer loans)	0.35%**	0.1%*	0.03%*	0.33%
Stock returns (avg. daily returns)	0.03%*	−0.01"%*	**	0.02%
Stock returns (std dev. of daily returns)	1.03%**	2.77%**	**	1.55%

(b) Institution type

	Local banks and Desjardins group	*Foreign banks*	*Credit unions*	*All*
Z-score (std dev. from default)	131.80	44.28	49.63	126.7421
Loan loss provisions (% of gross customer loans)	0.34%	0.39%	0.10%	0.33%
Stock returns (avg. daily returns)	0.02%			0.02%
Stock returns (std dev. of daily returns)	1.55%			1.55%

Source: Author

Notes: All figures are the weighted averages values for the relevant sub-sample. The independence of clusters was tested using non-parametric equality-of-weighted averages two-sample tests at 5% significance. According to the results of these tests, the number of asterisks (*, ** or ***) stands for the statistical difference of any given cluster/ownership structure from that number of other clusters/ownership structures for that indicator. For example, two asterisks (**) imply that the cluster is statistically different from two (furthest) business models but not the third (closest) one. See Appendix G for the assumptions pertaining to the construction of the net stable funding ratio (NSFR) measure largest for diversified retail banks, followed by the focused retail. The high Z-scores are driven by local banks. These banks seem to be more resilient than the foreign and investment banks that exhibit much lower Z-scores. The loan loss provisions confirm this result.

To conclude, the risk assessed using accounting and market indicators differ per business models, ownership structure and size of banks and credit unions during the periods of analysis in Europe, US and Canada.

Generally, retail-oriented banks whether diversified (type 1) or focused are farthest from default in Europe and Canada. On the opposite, the investment banks fared better in the US as compared to the other business models but not when compared to the retail-oriented credit unions. However, it is worth nothing that the distance to default of US banks is generally lower (20) than their European (43.7) and Canadian (126) counterparts. This shows higher probability of default for US banks, followed by the European banks.

Monitoring the evolution of risk per business model, size and ownership structure is important to assess the resilience of the sum of components of the financial system and its capacity to withstand an external shock. The risk metrics used should be also considered in the financial stability assessment.

References

Ayadi, R. et al. (2016), "Banking Business Models Monitor 2015: Europe", Montreal, International Research Centre on Cooperative Finance, HEC Montreal.

Ayadi, R. et al. (2017), "Bank and Credit Unions Business Models in the United States", Montreal, International Research Centre on Cooperative Finance, HEC Montreal.

CHAPTER 10

Regulation and Business Models

Banks (and credit unions) in Europe,[1] US[2] and Canada are regulated entities. The regulatory authorities adopt and adapt the Basel global standards to their financial systems to ensure that banks are sound and resilient. Banks are required to operate with a minimum capital requirement, hold sufficient liquid assets and to be resilient to extreme shock scenarios. Credit unions are also regulated using equivalent approach but generally much less stringency applies in the conduct of business.

Depending on their business models, ownership structure and size, banks and other financial institutions respond differently to regulation and regulatory metrics that are not calibrated to their business models. The differences in their response contribute to better understand the stability and safety of the financial system.

[1] See Ayadi et al. (2012), Ayadi and Resti (2004).

[2] The regulation and supervision of banks and credit unions in the US differ. Banks are regulated by three different federal authorities, depending on whether they are federally or state chartered: the Office of the Comptroller of the Currency (OCC) regulates depository banks that have a federal charter; state-chartered banks are regulated by state regulators, by the Federal Reserve (for those that choose to be members of the Federal Reserve System) and by the Federal Deposit Insurance Corporation (FDIC). All federally chartered credit unions are regulated and supervised by the National Credit Union Administration (NCUA), while state-chartered credit unions are also supervised at the state level. While the three banking supervisors coordinate their regulatory initiatives very closely, credit union regulation can often differ more. In general, credit union capital requirements follow broadly similar principles to those of banks. For more details, see Appendix G.

R. Ayadi, *Banking Business Models*, Palgrave Macmillan Studies in Banking and Financial Institutions,
https://doi.org/10.1007/978-3-030-02248-8_10

This chapter exposes the regulatory indicators used and shows the results of how business models of banks and credit unions in Europe, US and Canada respond to regulation.

10.1 Regulatory Indicators

Several regulatory indicators are used to assess how business models respond to regulation. These indicators have been tested in Ayadi et al. (2011, 2012, 2016a, 2017) and Ayadi and de Groen (2014).

Risk-weighted assets (RWA) (% of assets), or the average risk weights, provide a regulatory measure of risk. Banks with higher RWA are expected to be more sensitive to risks and are thus required to hold more/less regulatory capital to account for their risk-weighted balance sheet, without counting the risk pertaining to the off-balance sheet.[3] The RWA metric is the basis of Basel regulation, provided that the risk weights are measured correctly. The RWA to total asset should be an indicator of portfolio risk that reflects the true risk profile of the bank's balance sheet and off-balance sheet. However, due to the multiplicity of the models (e.g. standard, foundation and internal rating-based models) and the politically driven policies (e.g. risk weights on sovereign exposure) to measure the risk weights, there is a concern of regulatory arbitrage that has put into question the RWA metric.

The closest concept for credit unions is the **risk-based net worth (RBNW) ratio**. This is a risk-weighted average of on and off-balance sheet items, reported as a share of the total assets of a credit union.

Tier 1 capital ratio: It reflects the loss absorption capacity of banks under the Basel capital rules. For any given level of risk, holding more capital could, in principle, imply a greater stability. This indicator only applies to banks.

Tangible common equity: Total equity capital excluding minority interests, adjusted for preferred stocks, goodwill and other intangibles. Mortgage servicing rights are not treated as intangible assets.

Leverage ratio (or equity ratio): Tangible common equity over total assets. The higher this ratio, the more stable the bank.

The closest concept for credit unions is the **net worth ratio** (i.e. largely retained earnings as a share of total assets). Higher levels of net worth indicate that the credit union has a higher loss-absorbing capacity.

[3] The off-balance sheet exposures could not be included in because of unavailability of data.

Supervisory capital assessments, such as the asset quality review and stress test performed by the European Banking Authority (EBA), show the resilience capacity of banks to extreme shocks. This exercise is only done for Europe.

Net stable funding ratio (NSFR): This is the available stable funding/required stable funding. For the full definition and computation, see Appendix G. This indicator only applies to banks.

An alternative assessment of default risks follows the "top-down" approach to calibrating regulatory minimum capital requirements under stress conditions, as described in BCBS (2010). This method allows for assessing the resilience of banks per business model to external shocks. More specifically, the quantiles of the return to risk-weighted assets (RoRWA) are used to construct expected losses that banks may face under a stress scenario. If the most loss-absorbing parts of equity (i.e. the tangible common capital ratio) remain below or close to such a measure, then the likelihood of a default would be equally higher under those stress conditions.

As an illustrative example, consider a bank that achieves 3% RoRWA in normal years. Let us assume that in a bad year, which occurs randomly once every 20 years, the bank faces a 7% loss. Note that the loss corresponds precisely to the 5th percentile of the distribution function. Although effective average earnings of 2.5% RoRWA may be considered healthy, the bank will nevertheless default if its risk-adjusted capital level is below 7% in a bad year. Assuming a similar distribution for other banks, the regulators should ensure that the banks have at least this amount of capital at all times to cope with stress conditions when needed.

10.2 Regulation and Business Models in Europe

The empirical investigation in Ayadi et al. (2016a) summarises the key regulatory and supervisory indicators in Table 10.1 and Appendix F.

The regulatory capital ratios suggest that the retail-oriented banks respond with significantly higher median risk weights than the wholesale and investment banks. The latter exhibits significantly higher Tier 1 ratios thanks to relatively lower RWAs. Taken both indicators together, the wholesale banks respond with higher (tangible common) equity and the investment banks with the lowest levels (below the median values). If data on off-balance sheet exposures is available, this can provide additional information on the level of risk per business model.

Table 10.1 Regulatory and supervisory indicators in Europe

(a) Business models

	Focused retail	*Diversified retail (type 1)*	*Diversified retail (type 2)*	*Wholesale*	*Investment*	*All*
Risk-weighted assets (RWA) (% of assets)	62.3%***	56.9%****	62.8%***	42.3%****	37.9%****	57.6%
Tier 1 capital ratio (% of RWA)	12.5%**	12.6%***	12.2%***	18.6%****	15.2%****	12.8%
Tang. common eq. (% of tang. assets)	6.7%****	6.2%****	7.2%****	9.7%****	5.7%****	6.5%
AQR 2014–2015 impact (% of RWA)	−0.7%	−0.4%	−0.4%	−0.0%	−0.1%	−0.3%
Stress test 2014–2015 impact (% of RWA)	−3.0%	−2.3%	−2.4%	−0.9%	−1.7%	−2.3%
Shortfall (% of RWA)	0.0%*	0.0%	0.0%	0.0%	0.0%*	0.0%
NSFR (Avail./req. funding)	106.9%****	119%****	93.3%****	241.8%****	131.9%****	111.1%

(b) Ownership structures

	Commercial	*Cooperative*	*Nationalised*	*Public*	*Savings*	*All*
Risk-weighted assets (RWA) (% assets)	58.5%**	58.7%**	56.4%*	49.9%****	57.1%***	57.7%
Tier 1 capital ratio (% of RWA)	13.3%***	12.3%****	9.9%****	14.7%****	13.1%***	12.8%
Tang. common eq. (% of tang. assets)	8.2%****	6.3%****	3.7%****	7.6%****	6.1%****	6.5%
AQR 2014–2015 impact (% of RWA)	−0.2%	−0.6%	−0.4%	−0.2%	−0.2%	−0.3%
Stress test 2014–2015 impact (% of RWA)	−1.9%	−2.8%	−5.6%*	−1.0%*	−1.8%	−2.3%
Shortfall (% of RWA)	0.0%	0.0%	0.0%	0.0%	0.0%	0.0%
NSFR (Avail./req. funding)	119.4%****	110.7%****	91.6%****	105.5%****	109.7%****	111.1%

Source: Reproduced from Ayadi et al. (2016a)

Notes: All figures are the median values for the relevant sub-sample. The independence of clusters/ownership structures was tested using non-parametric equality-of-medians two-sample tests at 5% significance. According to the results of these tests, the number of asterisks (*, **, *** or ****) stands for the statistical difference of any given cluster/ownership structure from that number of other clusters/ownership structures for that indicator. For example, two asterisks (**) imply that the cluster/ownership structure is statistically different from two (furthest) business models/ownership structures but not the two (closest) ones. See Appendix G for the assumptions pertaining to the construction of the net stable funding ratio (NSFR) measure

Among the ownership structures, the median average risk weights are close to the sample median, except for the public banks. The latter, however, have the highest risk-weighted capital ratios, owing to the lowest RWA level. Overall, the nationalised banks have the weakest capital position and the commercial banks exhibit the highest tangible common equity as a percentage of total assets—which can reflect on their relatively lower leveraging position as compared to the others.

The results of the supervisory capital assessments, like the asset quality review and stress test performed by the European Banking Authority,[4] show higher adjustments and provisions for risks for the retail-oriented banks. The median values are, however, not significant. Also, across ownership structures, the results are mostly insignificant, though nationalised banks seem to have incurred significantly higher stress test provisions than the public banks.

The liquidity ratios of the market-funded oriented business models are significantly higher than the retail-funded oriented models. The differences across ownership structures are less apparent. Except for the nationalised banks, the median values are all above the future requirement of 100%.

To assess the resilience of business models under stress event, Fig. 10.1 provides an illustration of the distribution of the risk-weighted returns for all banks and years in the sample. The highest frequency of the distribution is around 1% RoRWA, implying healthy returns for most banks in normal years. Assuming that a bad year is defined as a once-in-a-10-year event, that is, lower 10th percentile losses, banks face no losses (see Fig. 10.2 and Table 10.2). If a bad year is defined to be a rarer and, thus, a more destructive event, that is, lower 5th percentile, the potential losses increase to 1.7%.[5] However, the potential losses increase faced by wholesale and investment banks, and similarly by nationalised and commercial banks are much higher than the average of 1.7% faced by all banks.

Commercial banks and, understandably, nationalised banks are subject to more losses than others in extreme stress conditions. This result may suggest that these types of banks are intrinsically more risky and less

[4] Assessment performed a sub-sample of 200 European banks.

[5] Assuming that earnings are randomly and independently distributed, the estimates would imply that a bank with risk-adjusted capital less than 1.7% would face a default likelihood of 5% at any given point in time. However, the earnings distributions of different banks are typically highly correlated, especially when interbank activities and common exposures are substantial. It is also assumed that losses are not correlated over time, which is also not likely to be the case. Based on these shortcomings, the actual default likelihoods are likely to be much higher than the levels implied by the percentile estimates.

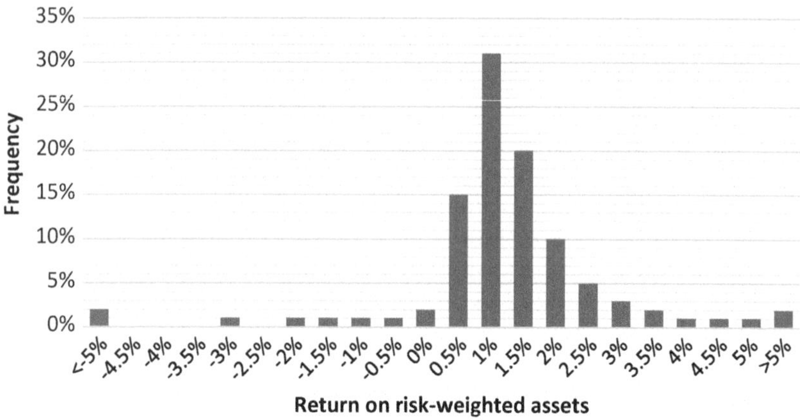

Fig. 10.1 Distribution of risk-weighted returns (RoRWA) in Europe. Source: Reproduced from Ayadi et al. (2016a). Note: This figure depicts the distribution for all banks covered in the study for the years from 2005 to 2014

resilient than other types of banks such as saving banks and cooperatives banks, which exhibit much lower losses in extreme stress conditions.

Using such estimates[6] for different business models and ownership structures, one can assess the adequacy of the capital requirements to cope with stress conditions. The lower percentile estimates depicted in Table 10.2 provide an insight into the losses that banks in Europe have faced in recent years. When the entire sample is considered, the risk-adjusted losses, as measured by RoRWA, are approximately 8.0% at the 1st percentile. However, the depicted period had a large impact on returns. Losses were substantially greater during the financial and economic crises years than during the pre-crises period, with the pooled sample of banks having faced risk-adjusted 1st percentile losses of respectively 8.1% and 0.9%.[7]

[6] Ayadi et al. (2016a) applied the distribution-free quantile estimator, first proposed by Harrell and Davis (1982), to generate alternative estimates for the lower percentiles, in addition to the statistics obtained from the original sample. Harrell and Davis (1982) provide a kernel quantile estimator in which the order statistics (i.e. smallest observations) used in traditional non-parametric estimators are given the greatest weight. The estimation results should, nevertheless, be interpreted with caution due to potential estimation errors.

[7] Although the estimates for different years can clearly not be used to build the scenarios, the substantial differences highlight the need for balanced data. The extent to which the crisis years are included in the dataset has a substantial impact on the severity of the stress scenarios and the relevant capital requirements.

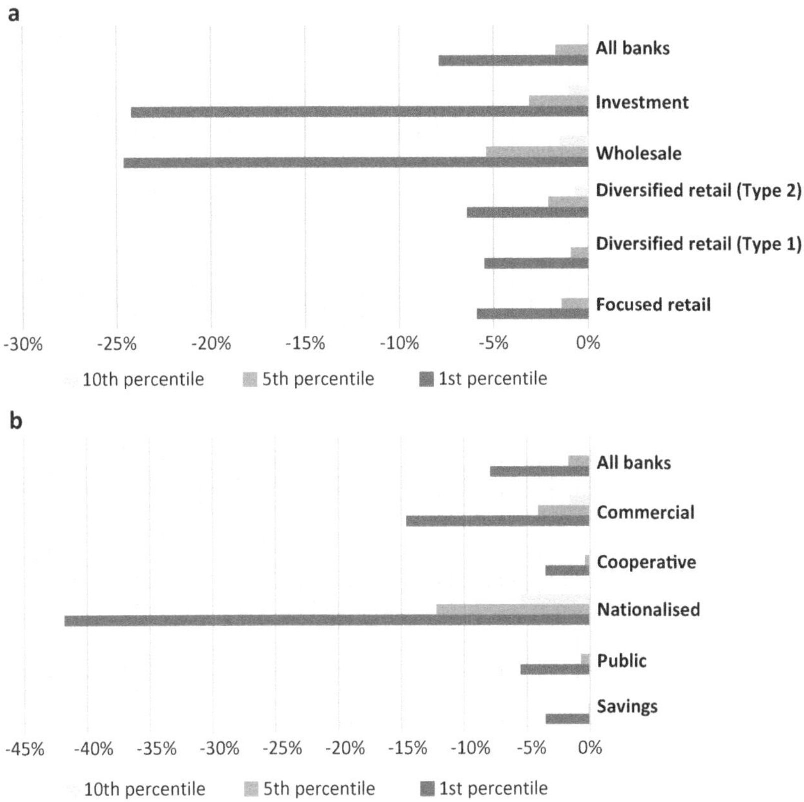

Fig. 10.2 Return on risk-weighted assets (RoRWA) (top percentiles). (**a**) Business models (**b**) Ownership structure. Source: Reproduced from Ayadi et al. (2016a). Note: This figure depicts the RoRWA of the top percentiles (1st, 5th and 10th) for all banks covered in the study for the years from 2005 to 2014. The dotted lines show the minimum regulatory requirements under CRDIV, common equity Tier 1 (CET1) requirement of 4.5%, Tier 1 requirement of 6% and total capital requirement (TCR) of 8% respectively

Looking at results by business models, it is shown that, following the financial crisis, both wholesale and investment banks are suffering greater losses at the 1st percentile, as compared to the retail-oriented banks,

Table 10.2 Lower percentile estimates for return on risk-weighted assets (RoRWA)

(a) Business models

		Sample statistics			*Harrell-Davis estimates*		
	Obs	*1st*	*5th*	*10th*	*1st*	*5th*	*10th*
All years (2005–2014)							
Model 1—Focus. retail	2728	−5.9%	−1.4%	0.1%	−6.0%	−1.4%	0.1%
Model 2—Div. retail (type 1)	3958	−5.5%	−0.9%	0.2%	−5.7%	−0.9%	0.2%
Model 3—Div. retail (type 2)	1920	−6.4%	−2.1%	−0.7%	−6.6%	−2.1%	−0.7%
Model 4—Wholesale	588	−24.6%	−5.4%	−1.5%	−29.7%	−6.0%	−1.6%
Model 5—Investment	896	−25.9%	−3.1%	−1.0%	−24.5%	−3.1%	−1.0%
All banks	10,254	−7.9%	−1.7%	0.0%	−8.0%	−1.7%	0.0%
Pre crisis (2005–2006)							
Model 1—Focus. retail	92	−2.4%	0.5%	0.9%	−1.9%	0.3%	0.9%
Model 2—Div. retail (type 1)	79	−0.6%	0.5%	1.0%	−0.3%	0.5%	1.0%
Model 3—Div. retail (type 2)	163	0.1%	0.5%	0.7%	0.1%	0.5%	0.7%
Model 4—Wholesale	18	−24.6%	−24.6%	−24.5%	−24.3%	−21.9%	−15.8%
Model 5—Investment	39	0.3%	0.3%	0.9%	0.3%	0.5%	0.8%
All banks	410	−0.9%	0.4%	0.8%	−4.2%	0.4%	0.8%
Fin. crisis (2007–2009)							
Model 1—Focus. retail	314	−3.8%	−1.6%	0.0%	−4.3%	−1.5%	−0.1%
Model 2—Div. retail (type 1)	174	−5.7%	−2.7%	−0.9%	−7.2%	−2.7%	−1.0%
Model 3—Div. retail (type 2)	330	−4.7%	−1.9%	−0.3%	−7.1%	−1.9%	−0.4%
Model 4—Wholesale	47	−15.5%	−12.1%	−4.1%	−15.2%	−11.6%	−5.4%
Model 5—Investment	92	−8.5%	−1.9%	−1.5%	−7.7%	−2.8%	−1.5%
All banks	988	−7.1%	−2.0%	−0.7%	−7.1%	−2.1%	−0.7%
Econ. crisis (2010–2012)							
Model 1—Focus. retail	1414	−6.4%	−1.5%	0.1%	−6.7%	−1.5%	0.1%
Model 2—Div. retail (type 1)	2199	−5.5%	−0.5%	0.3%	−5.8%	−0.6%	0.3%
Model 3—Div. retail (type 2)	953	−4.7%	−2.0%	−0.6%	−5.4%	−1.9%	−0.6%
Model 4—Wholesale	337	−14.0%	−5.3%	−2.2%	−15.1%	−5.1%	−2.0%
Model 5—Investment	435	−29.6%	−3.5%	−1.2%	−32.9%	−4.5%	−1.3%
All banks	5404	−8.1%	−1.7%	0.0%	−8.4%	−1.7%	0.0%
Fin + econ crises (2007–2012)							
Model 1—Focus. retail	1728	−6.2%	−1.5%	0.1%	−6.4%	−1.5%	0.1%
Model 2—Div. retail (type 1)	2373	−5.5%	−0.8%	0.2%	−5.8%	−0.9%	0.2%
Model 3—Div. retail (type 2)	1283	−4.7%	−1.9%	−0.5%	−5.2%	−1.9%	−0.6%
Model 4—Wholesale	384	−14.7%	−5.4%	−2.2%	−15.3%	−5.8%	−2.1%
Model 5—Investment	527	−25.9%	−3.5%	−1.3%	−28.1%	−3.8%	−1.4%
All banks	6392	−8.1%	−1.9%	−0.1%	−8.1%	−1.8%	−0.1%
Post crisis (2013–2014)							
Model 1—Focus. retail	908	−5.6%	−1.7%	0.1%	−5.8%	−1.5%	0.1%
Model 2—Div. retail (type 1)	1506	−6.0%	−1.0%	0.2%	−6.0%	−1.0%	0.2%
Model 3—Div. retail (type 2)	474	−11.3%	−3.2%	−1.6%	−20.2%	−3.3%	−1.6%

(*continued*)

Table 10.2 (continued)

(a) Business models

	Obs	Sample statistics 1st	5th	10th	Harrell-Davis estimates 1st	5th	10th
Model 4—Wholesale	186	−76.9%	−3.8%	−0.7%	−100.4%	−6.7%	−0.8%
Model 5—Investment	330	−21.9%	−2.9%	−0.6%	−23.9%	−2.8%	−0.6%
All banks	3452	−8.4%	−1.8%	−0.1%	−8.6%	−1.8%	−0.1%

(b) Ownership structures

	Obs	Sample statistics 1st	5th	10th	Harrell-Davis estimates 1st	5th	10th
All years (2005–2014)							
Commercial	2994	−14.6%	−4.1%	−1.6%	−15.2%	−4.1%	−1.6%
Cooperative	4109	−3.5%	−0.4%	0.2%	−3.5%	−0.4%	0.2%
Nationalised	252	−41.8%	−12.2%	−5.5%	−38.8%	−13.2%	−6.0%
Public	373	−5.5%	−0.7%	0.2%	−7.3%	−0.9%	0.2%
Savings	2526	−3.5%	−0.1%	0.2%	−3.3%	−0.1%	0.2%
All banks	10,254	−7.9%	−1.7%	0.0%	−8.0%	−1.7%	0.0%
Pre crisis (2005–2006)							
Commercial	211	−2.4%	0.5%	0.9%	−14.4%	0.4%	0.9%
Cooperative	53	0.2%	0.3%	0.5%	0.2%	0.3%	0.6%
Nationalised	40	−1.4%	0.0%	0.7%	−1.2%	−0.2%	0.5%
Public	20	0.1%	0.2%	0.5%	0.1%	0.2%	0.4%
Savings	86	0.2%	0.5%	0.7%	0.2%	0.5%	0.7%
All banks	410	−0.9%	0.4%	0.8%	−4.2%	0.4%	0.8%
Fin. crisis (2007–2009)							
Commercial	470	−10.8%	−2.7%	−1.0%	−11.4%	−2.8%	−1.0%
Cooperative	143	−2.2%	−1.1%	0.1%	−2.1%	−1.0%	0.0%
Nationalised	76	−7.1%	−3.5%	−2.7%	−6.6%	−3.9%	−2.7%
Public	73	−4.1%	−0.3%	0.3%	−3.5%	−0.6%	0.2%
Savings	226	−4.7%	−1.1%	−0.1%	−4.5%	−1.2%	−0.2%
All banks	988	−7.1%	−2.0%	−0.7%	−7.1%	−2.1%	−0.7%
Econ. crisis (2010–2012)							
Commercial	1412	−14.4%	−4.8%	−2.2%	−16.0%	−4.9%	−2.2%
Cooperative	2395	−2.8%	0.0%	0.3%	−2.8%	0.0%	0.3%
Nationalised	86	−49.0%	−21.9%	−12.2%	−45.9%	−24.0%	−13.0%
Public	167	−6.5%	−1.2%	0.2%	−6.8%	−1.5%	0.1%
Savings	1344	−3.5%	−0.1%	0.2%	−3.4%	−0.1%	0.2%
All banks	5404	−8.1%	−1.7%	0.0%	−8.4%	−1.7%	0.0%
Fin + econ crises (2007–2012)							
Commercial	1882	−14.3%	−4.5%	−1.8%	−14.4%	−4.4%	−1.8%
Cooperative	2538	−2.6%	0.0%	0.3%	−2.7%	0.0%	0.3%

(*continued*)

Table 10.2 (continued)

(b) Ownership structures

		Sample statistics			Harrell-Davis estimates		
	Obs	*1st*	*5th*	*10th*	*1st*	*5th*	*10th*
Nationalised	162	−45.8%	−12.2%	−6.1%	−40.9%	−14.0%	−6.6%
Public	240	−4.1%	−0.6%	0.2%	−5.6%	−1.0%	0.2%
Savings	1570	−3.8%	−0.3%	0.1%	−3.7%	−0.3%	0.1%
All banks	6392	−8.1%	−1.9%	−0.1%	−8.1%	−1.8%	−0.1%
Post crisis (2013–2014)							
Commercial	901	−19.1%	−4.1%	−1.7%	−21.8%	−4.1%	−1.7%
Cooperative	1518	−4.9%	−1.1%	0.2%	−5.1%	−1.1%	0.2%
Nationalised	50	−41.8%	−21.9%	−9.4%	−38.6%	−22.2%	−12.1%
Public	113	−5.5%	−1.8%	0.1%	−37.4%	−1.7%	0.0%
Savings	870	−2.4%	0.0%	0.3%	−3.0%	0.0%	0.3%
All banks	3452	−8.4%	−1.8%	−0.1%	−8.6%	−1.8%	−0.1%

Source: Reproduced from Ayadi et al. (2016a)

Note: The figures correspond to the 1st, 5th and 10th percentile estimates of the distribution of the RoRWA, conditional on the business models/ownership structures and time periods across the sample

regardless of the statistical procedure used.[8] This leads to question the resilience of these two business models when they are facing extreme stress conditions. In 2013–2014, it seems that the investment banks fare relatively better than wholesale banks in terms of their capacity to withstand extreme shocks, although both are driving the overall sample to levels of losses much above retail-oriented banks all together. However, such a finding must be closely monitored annually to form a view on the long-term resilience of business models in banks.

These results are important evidence showing that during this period of investigation, retail-oriented banks, cooperative and savings banks are more resilient than wholesale, investment and commercial banks. Nationalised banks are, understandably, not resilient and hence should be dealt with by the respective governments or resolution authorities to avoid future detrimental impact on financial stability.

A more dynamic analysis shows that the order in peak losses differs substantially for the different sub-periods in the sample. During the pre-crisis years 2005 and 2006, losses occurred only for the 1st percentile

[8] It is difficult to make a firm statement due to the low data coverage before 2007.

while, during the crises, losses were observed in the 10th percentile and below. The losses climbed gradually during the crises. During the 2007–2009 financial crisis, the losses were less than during the 2010–2012 Eurozone economic crisis.

The order of the business models is also shifted. Looking at the 1st percentile, the investment banks reported losses below those of the wholesale banks during the financial crisis, while the investment banks reported the highest losses during the economic crisis. The focused retail banks, furthermore, clearly lost more during the economic crisis than during the financial crisis, while the losses of the diversified retail banks were fairly similar during both crises. As expected, the losses of all business models deteriorated in the aftermath of the crises.

The order of the ownership structures remained the same, except for nationalised and public banks. In fact, the peak losses of both ownership structures increased substantially between the financial and economic crises. Moreover, the peak losses diverged in the aftermath of the crises. The peak losses of the commercial banks with higher losses during the financial crisis increased during the first two years after the crisis, while the peak losses of the savings banks with the lowest RoRWA during the crises decreased.

The dynamic analysis of the different crisis periods shows that diversity of business models and ownership structures can be a factor of resilience, as the capacity of different business models and ownership structures to withstand extreme stress conditions differ, depending on the nature of the crisis and, hence, the overall banking system remains afloat. In this analysis and at least in this period of investigation, retail-oriented banks, savings and cooperatives banks have provided systemic resilience to the European banking sector. Conversely, investment, wholesale and commercial banks have dragged the overall banking system to levels of losses in extreme stress conditions.

Another dimension is the comparison of the mean values for RoRWAs (Table 10.3), which shows that the distinctions are fairly insignificant for the pre-crisis and financial crisis period when tested using Wilcoxon-Mann-Whitney non-parametric two-sample tests. Indeed, for the period between 2005 and 2009, far fewer observations were available. The results for all years show that the wholesale and investment banks, on average, reported distinctly higher RoRWAs than banks belonging to one of the retail-oriented models. Looking at all the crises years (2007–2012), the wholesale banks are still significantly better performing, while the

Table 10.3 Mean RoRWA

(a) Business models

	Focused retail	*Diversified retail (type 1)*	*Diversified retail (type 2)*	*Wholesale*	*Investment*	*All*
All years (2005–2014)	0.89%***	0.82%***	0.62%****	1.5%***	1.15%***	0.87%
Pre crisis (2005–2006)	1.6%**	2.51%***	1.79%**	2.49%*	3.09%**	2.05%
Financial crisis (2007–2009)	1%	0.98%	0.8%	0.98%	1.52%	0.98%
Economic crisis (2010–2012)	0.76%****	0.78%****	0.61%****	2.37%***	0.69%***	0.84%
Crises years (2007–2012)	0.81%****	0.79%****	0.66%****	2.2%***	0.84%***	0.86%
Post crisis (2013–2014)	0.98%***	0.78%***	0.11%****	−0.05%***	1.41%***	0.76%

(b) Ownership structures

	Commercial	*Cooperative*	*Nationalised*	*Public*	*Savings*	*All*
All years (2005–2014)	0.88%***	0.88%****	−1.59%****	1.15%***	1.06%****	0.88%
Pre crisis (2005–2006)	2.32%**	1.73%*	1.71%	2.12%	1.73%*	2.05%
Financial crisis (2007–2009)	1.03%*	0.90%*	0.22%**	1.48%**	0.94%	0.96%
Economic crisis (2010–2012)	0.72%*	0.97%**	−4.06%****	1.31%***	1.01%**	0.85%
Crises years (2007–2012)	0.80%**	0.97%***	−2.05%****	1.36%***	1.00%**	0.86%
Post crisis (2013–2014)	0.73%**	0.71%***	−2.74%****	0.54%*	1.11%**	0.76%

Source: Reproduced from Ayadi et al. (2016a)

Notes: All figures are the mean values for all banks in the sample. The independence of clusters/ownership structures was tested using Wilcoxon-Mann-Whitney non-parametric two-sample tests at 5% significance. The number of asterisks (*, **, ***, ****) stands for the statistical difference of any given cluster from that number of other clusters/ownership structures for that indicator. For example, a single asterisk (*) implies that the clusters/ownership structure is statistically different from the furthest clusters/ownership structure but not the other three diversified retail (type 2) banks reported the average lowest RoRWAs. In the aftermath of the crisis, both wholesale and diversified retail (type 2) banks were performing significantly worse than the other three business models.

The averages for the different ownership structures show that the nationalised banks were the only ones reporting losses for the entire sample period. In turn, the public and savings banks reported the significantly highest returns. The remaining results are, except for the nationalised banks, in most cases not significant.

The findings show clear distinctions across business models and ownership structures in terms of peak losses, which suggest that the average risk weights do not reflect the underlying risks of certain banks. In particular, wholesale and investment banks faced severe default risks during the financial and economic crises. Nevertheless, these differences appear in the underlying risks, not in the average risk weights.[9]

10.3 Regulation and Business Models in the US

The empirical investigation in Ayadi et al. (2017) summarises the key regulatory and supervisory indicators in Table 10.4 and Appendix F.

The regulatory capital ratios for banks suggest that retail-oriented banks have significantly higher average risk weights than wholesale-oriented and investment-oriented banks. In turn, the latter business models have significantly higher Tier 1 and total capital ratios due to the lower RWA.

Considering the leverage ratio, investment-oriented banks have the least leverage (i.e. total assets over tangible common equity) and wholesale-

[9] Ayadi et al. (2011, 2012, 2016a) and Ayadi and De Groen (2014) provide evidence of a negative relationship between average risk weights and a number of risk factors for the EU's top banks in recent years, including estimates of default likelihood, Tier 1 ratio and earnings volatility. Supplemental evidence from the study also shows that investment-oriented banks may have found ways to take on more risk than their regulatory risk measures would reflect. Das and Sy (2012) have shown that banks with lower average risk weights (measured by the risk-weighted assets to asset ratio) do a poor job in predicting market measures of risk, especially during the crisis. The Basel Committee on Banking Supervision (2013) conducted a benchmarking exercise, using data for more than 100 banks, which showed that there are large differences between the internal models used to determine the risk-weighted assets (see BCBS (2013)). More recently, using a sample of European banks, Ayadi et al. (2016b) explain the differences in bank risk levels by the adoption of the internal risk-based (IRB) approaches and the RWA dispersion. Their findings point to a systematic regulatory arbitrage by diversified retail type 2 banks.

Table 10.4 Regulatory and supervisory indicators in the US

(a) Bank business models

	Model 1—Wholesale oriented	*Model 2—Retail (type 1)*	*Model 3—Retail (type 2)*	*Model 4—Investment oriented*	*All*
Risk-weighted assets (RWA) (% of assets)	64.83%***	72.81%***	82.33%***	58.82%***	72.19%
Tier 1 capital ratio (% of risk-weighted assets)	11.4%**	10.98%**	10.44%**	14.43%***	11.15%
Total regulatory capital (% of risk-weighted assets)	14.45%***	13.32%***	12.71%***	16.21%***	13.60%
Tangible common equity (% of tang. assets)	7.29%***	7.61%***	8.34%**	8.33%**	7.80%
NSFR (Avail./req. funding)	139.96%***	133.45%***	120.76%***	159.92%***	134.02%

(b) Bank size categories

	Micro (<1 bn)	*Very small (1–5 bn)*	*Small (5–10 bn)*	*Mid (10–50 bn)*	*Large (>50 bn)*	*All*
Risk-weighted assets (RWA) (% of assets)	69.28%***	72.26%**	69.45%***	72.33%**	72.83%**	72.19%
Tier 1 capital ratio (% of risk-weighted assets)	14.37%****	13.13%***	13.12%***	11.85%****	10.16%****	12.08%
Total regulatory capital (% of risk-weighted assets)	15.55%****	14.49%**	14.74%***	13.92%***	13.05%****	14.46%
Tangible common equity (% of tang. assets)	10%****	9.48%***	9.27%***	8.23%****	7.04%****	7.79%
NSFR (Avail./req. funding)	130.99%****	127.85%**	126.15%**	128.04%**	136.69%****	134.02%

(c) Credit union business models in the US

	Retail type 1	*Retail type 2*	*Retail type 3*	*All*
Net worth (% of assets)	10.27%**	11.34%**	13.77%**	10.83%
Risk-based net worth requirement	6.49%**	6.93%**	6.8%**	6.74%

Source: Reproduced from Ayadi et al. (2017)

Notes: All figures are weighted averages of the year-end observations. The independence of clusters (a.k.a. business models) and size categories was tested using Welch two-sample tests at 5% significance. To report the results of these tests, the number of asterisks (*, **, *** or ****) stands for the statistical difference of any given cluster/size category from that number of other clusters/size categories for that indicator. For example, two asterisks (**) in sub-table for business models imply that the business models are statistically different from the two (furthest) business models but not the third (closest) one oriented banks the highest. Among bank size categories, the average risk weights of very small, small and large banks are comparable and close to the sample average, while those of micro- and small banks are the lowest. In turn, generally, the capital ratios (Tier 1 capital and total regulatory capital) decrease with the size. This statement is also true for the leverage ratio.

For credit unions, the net worth ratio suggests that the retail type 3 have significantly higher median risk weights than retail type 2 and retail type 1 credit unions. In other words, retail type 3 credit unions have the least leverage.

The liquidity ratios (net stable funding ratios) only apply to the bank sample. The indicators suggest that the liquidity position of the market-oriented business models is higher than for the retail-oriented models. The differences across bank size categories are less apparent but, statistically, the micro and large banks have significantly higher NSFR than the intermediate-sized categories. The weighted averages are all well above the future requirement of 100%.

Looking at the distribution of RoRWA, Fig. 10.3 shows the distribution of the risk-weighted returns for all banks and years in the sample. The highest frequency of the distribution is around 2% RoRWA, implying healthy returns for most banks in normal years. Assuming that a bad year is defined as a once-in-a-10-year event, that is, lower 10th percentile return, banks face moderate losses of 0.4% (see also Fig. 10.4 and Table 10.5). If a bad

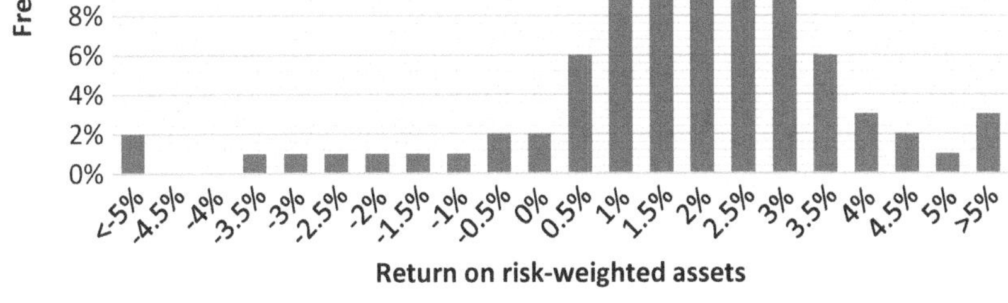

Fig. 10.3 Distribution of risk-weighted returns (RoRWA) in the US. Source: Reproduced from Ayadi et al. (2017). Note: This figure depicts the distribution for all banks covered in the study for the years from 2000 to 2014

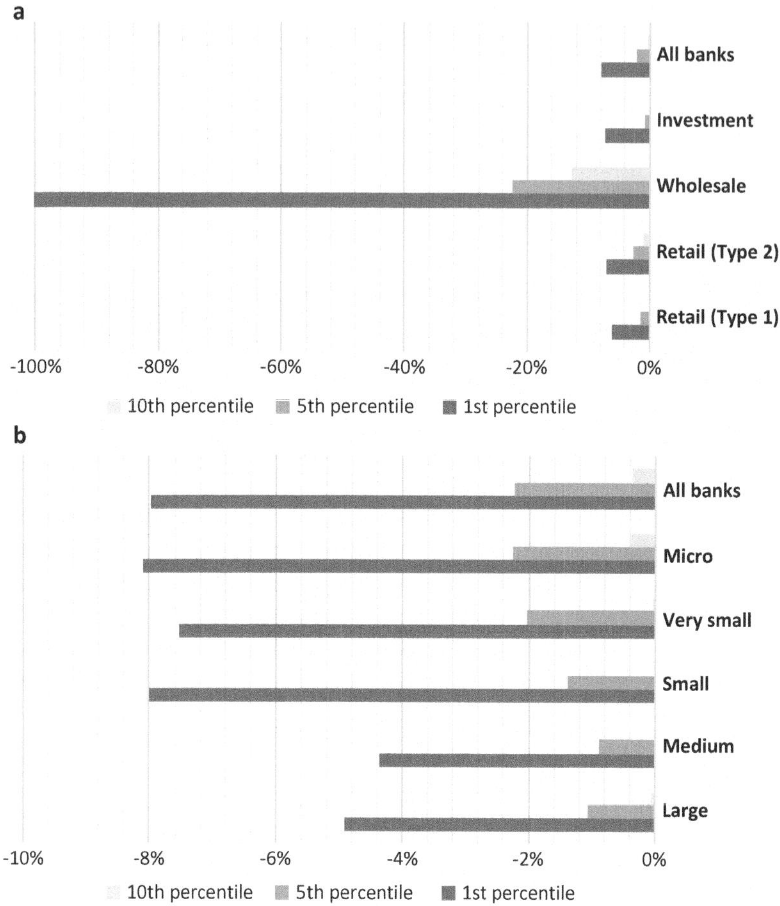

Fig. 10.4 Return on risk-weighted assets (top percentiles) in the US. (**a**) Bank business models (**b**) Bank size categories. Source: Reproduced from Ayadi et al. (2017). Note: This figure depicts the RoRWA of the top percentiles (1st, 5th and 10th) for all banks covered in the study for the years from 2000 to 2014. The dotted lines show the minimum regulatory requirements to be considered adequately capitalised by the FDIC; Tier 1 requirement of at least 4% and total capital requirement of at least 8% respectively

Table 10.5 Lower percentile estimates for return on risk-weighted assets (RoRWA) in the US

(a) Bank business models

	Obs.	*Sample statistics*		
		1st	*5th*	*10th*
All years (2000–2014)				
Model 1—Wholesale oriented	2664	−100.3%	−22.4%	−12.7%
Model 2—Retail (type 1)	41,993	−6.0%	−1.4%	0.1%
Model 3 —Retail (type 2)	48,738	−7.0%	−2.6%	−0.9%
Model 4—Investment oriented	14,828	−7.2%	−0.7%	0.4%
All banks	108,223	−8.0%	−2.2%	−0.4%
Pre crisis (2000–2006)				
Model 1—Wholesale oriented	1310	−51.7%	−21.2%	−14.7%
Model 2—Retail (type 1)	22,210	−5.1%	−0.3%	0.6%
Model 3—Retail (type 2)	23,822	−4.2%	−0.6%	0.4%
Model 4—Investment oriented	7593	−7.9%	−0.2%	0.7%
All banks	54,935	−6.7%	−0.7%	0.5%
Fin. crisis (2007–2009)				
Model 1—Wholesale oriented	601	−73.6%	−29.0%	−13.8%
Model 2—Retail (type 1)	6857	−9.1%	−3.5%	−1.3%
Model 3—Retail (type 2)	11,567	−9.9%	−4.8%	−2.8%
Model 4—Investment oriented	2218	−13.1%	−2.1%	−0.1%
All banks	21,243	−11.5%	−4.6%	−2.4%
Post crisis (2010–2014)				
Model 1—Wholesale oriented	753	−292.2%	−20.7%	−3.3%
Model 2—Retail (type 1)	12,926	−5.4%	−1.6%	−0.3%
Model 3—Retail (type 2)	13,349	−6.8%	−2.8%	−1.2%
Model 4—Investment oriented	5017	−5.3%	−0.7%	0.3%
All banks	32,045	−6.6%	−2.2%	−0.6%

(b) Bank size categories

	Obs.	*Sample statistics*		
		1st	*5th*	*10th*
All years (2000–2014)				
Micro (<1 bn)	100,427	−8.1%	−2.3%	−0.4%
Very small (1–5 bn)	5628	−7.5%	−2.0%	0.0%
Small (5–10 bn)	854	−8.0%	−1.4%	0.2%
Mid (10–50 bn)	908	−4.4%	−0.9%	0.4%
Large (>50 bn)	406	−4.9%	−1.1%	−0.1%
All banks	108,223	−8.0%	−2.2%	−0.4%

(continued)

Table 10.5 (continued)

(b) Bank size categories

	Obs.	*Sample statistics*		
		1st	*5th*	*10th*
Pre crisis (2000–2006)				
Micro (<1 bn)	51,711	−6.9%	−0.8%	0.4%
Very small (1–5 bn)	2246	−1.1%	0.7%	1.2%
Small (5–10 bn)	388	−1.7%	0.5%	1.0%
Mid (10–50 bn)	437	−0.9%	0.6%	1.0%
Large (>50 bn)	153	0.2%	0.6%	1.4%
All banks	54,935	−6.7%	−0.7%	0.5%
Fin. crisis (2007–2009)				
Micro (<1 bn)	19,653	−11.5%	−4.5%	−2.3%
Very small (1–5 bn)	1177	−13.1%	−6.4%	−3.7%
Small (5–10 bn)	167	−9.6%	−5.7%	−2.7%
Mid (10–50 bn)	152	−9.5%	−5.3%	−2.4%
Large (>50 bn)	94	−16.3%	−4.9%	−2.5%
All banks	21,243	−11.5%	−4.6%	−2.4%
Post crisis (2010–2014)				
Micro (<1 bn)	29,063	−6.7%	−2.3%	−0.6%
Very small (1–5 bn)	2205	−6.4%	−1.6%	0.0%
Small (5–10 bn)	299	−8.3%	−1.2%	0.4%
Mid (10–50 bn)	319	−2.9%	−0.2%	0.5%
Large (>50 bn)	159	−3.4%	−0.1%	0.7%
All banks	32,045	−6.6%	−2.2%	−0.6%

Source: Reproduced from Ayadi et al. (2017)

Note: The figures correspond to the 1st, 5th and 10th percentile estimates of the distribution of the RoRWA, conditional on the business models/bank size categories and time periods across the sample

year is defined as rarer and, thus, a more destructive event, that is, lower 5th percentile, the potential losses increase to 2.2%.

The lower percentile estimates depicted in Table 10.5 provide an insight into the losses that banks have faced in recent years. When the entire sample is considered, the risk-adjusted losses are approximately 8.0% at the 1st percentile. However, the depicted period had a large impact on returns. Losses were substantially greater during the financial crisis years than during the pre- and post-crises period, with the pooled sample of banks having faced risk-adjusted 1st percentile losses of respectively 6.7% and 6.6%, compared to 11.8% during the crisis.

Looking at results by business models, it is shown that, following the financial crisis, wholesale-oriented banks are suffering greater losses at the 1st percentile, as compared to the retail-oriented and investment-oriented banks. This leads to question the resilience of the wholesale-oriented business model when it is facing extreme stress conditions. Post-crisis, investment-oriented banks fare relatively better than all other business models. However, such a finding must be closely monitored annually to form a view on the long-term resilience of the business models of US banks.

As for the bank size categories, micro, very small and small banks are subject to more losses in extreme stress conditions than mid-sized and large banks. This result may suggest that the returns of smaller banks are either more volatile and/or more risky than for larger banks.

A similar dynamic analysis shows that the order in peak losses differs substantially for the different sub-periods in the sample. During the pre-crisis years from 2000 to 2006, losses occurred almost exclusively in the 1st and 5th percentile, while during the crisis even the 10th percentile was prone to losses. As expected, the losses of all business models during the aftermath of the crises recovered only slowly, leading to peak losses in between the pre-crisis and crisis levels.

The analysis of the different crisis periods shows that retail-oriented and investment-oriented banks, as well as mid-sized banks, have provided systemic resilience to the US banking sector. Conversely, wholesale-oriented and large banks have dragged the overall banking system to high levels of loss during the financial crisis.

The order of the bank size categories has changed during the period under review. Micro banks are among the most sensitive to extreme stress conditions before and after the financial crisis of 2007–2009. Also, pre- and post-crisis the two categories of largest banks (mid-sized and large banks) appear to be the most resilient. Noticeably, the large "systemically important" banks have incurred the highest losses during the financial crisis in the 1st percentile while, before the crisis, they came out as the most robust category. Overall, mid-sized banks have emerged over the 15 years under study as the most resilient, with contained peak losses in each period.

Another dimension is the comparison of the mean values for RoRWAs (Table 10.6), which shows that wholesale-oriented and investment-oriented banks, on average, reported distinctly higher RoRWAs than banks belonging to one of the retail-oriented models. Looking at all the financial

Table 10.6 Mean RoRWA

(a) Bank business models

	Model 1—Wholesale oriented	*Model 2—Retail (type 1)*	*Model 3—Retail (type 2)*	*Model 4—Investment oriented*	*All*
All years (2000–2014)	2.3%***	1.9%***	1.6%***	2.4%***	2.0%
Pre crisis (2000–2006)	3.0%***	2.4%***	2.3%***	3.2%***	2.6%
Financial crisis (2007–2009)	0.8%***	0.9%***	0.5%***	2.3%***	0.8%
Post crisis (2010–2014)	2.8%***	1.8%***	1.7%***	2.0%***	2.1%

(b) Bank size categories

	Micro (<1 bn)	*Very small (1–5 bn)*	*Small (5–10 bn)*	*Mid (10–50 bn)*	*Large (>50 bn)*	*All*
All years (2000–2014)	1.8%***	3.1%***	3.6%**	2.5%***	1.7%*	2.0%
Pre crisis (2000–2006)	2.4%****	2.9%*	6.1%*	2.8%*	2.2%*	2.6%
Financial crisis (2007–2009)	0.9%	1.0%	0.6%	1.9%	0.6%	0.8%
Post crisis (2010–2014)	1.4%****	4.4%***	2.0%**	2.5%**	1.9%*	2.1%

Source: Reproduced from Ayadi et al. (2017)

Notes: All figures are the mean values for all banks in the business models/bank size category. The independence of business models/bank size categories was tested using Wilcoxon-Mann-Whitney non-parametric two-sample tests at 5% significance. The number of asterisks (*, **, ***, ****) stands for the statistical difference of any given business model/size category from that number of other business models/bank size categories for that indicator. For example, two asterisks (**) in sub-table imply that the business model is statistically different from the two (furthest) business models but not the third (closest) one

crisis years (2007–2009), investment-oriented banks are by far the best performing, while retail (type 2) banks reported the lowest average RoRWAs. Post-crisis, wholesale-oriented and investment-oriented banks were performing significantly better than retail-oriented business models.

The averages for the different bank sizes show that no size category has reported losses for the entire sample period or in any of the three sub-periods. The lowest mean returns of 0.6% were reported during the financial crisis by small and large banks. Large banks that looked most resilient, based on the peak losses reported, on average, the lowest average RoRWA. These low RoRWA were, however, not significantly different from those of small banks. Micro banks that reported the highest peak losses are also in the lower echelons when comparing the averages.

Similarly to the findings in Europe, the findings in the US show clear distinctions across business models and bank size categories in terms of peak losses, which suggest that the average risk weights—which are the denominators of RoRWA—do not reflect the underlying risks of certain banks in the clusters. In particular, wholesale-oriented banks faced severe default risks during the financial crisis. Nevertheless, these differences appear in the underlying risks, not in the average risk weights.[10]

Turning to credit unions, capital requirements over the period of 15 years under review consist of balance sheet size capital requirements per total assets and a risk-sensitive ratio, which only applies for large, "complex" institutions. By and large, most credit unions in the US may only count retained earnings towards their capital requirements. While credit union capital requirements had historically been more lenient, in 1998 the Congress established today's balance sheet size capital requirements (per total assets) for most credit unions and directed the NCUA to implement an additional risk-based net worth requirement for larger, more complex credit unions.

The balance sheet size capital requirement for a credit union is its **net worth ratio** (i.e. largely retained earnings as a share of total assets). Higher levels of net worth indicate that the credit union has a higher loss-absorbing capacity. The NCUA considers that non-complex credit unions are well capitalised when they maintain a minimum net worth to assets ratio above 7.0%, adequately capitalised when the ratio is above 6.0% and undercapitalised when it falls below that threshold.

Figure 10.5 shows that, across business models, average net worth ratio was more than sufficient for credit unions to be considered well capitalised, assuming they are not complex. For all three business models, average net worth decreased between 2000 and 2003 and rose in the years before the crisis. During the crisis, the average net worth ratio deteriorated and remained fairly stable in the aftermath of the crisis. Retail type 3 credit unions had the highest average net worth ratio throughout the

[10] See footnote 9.

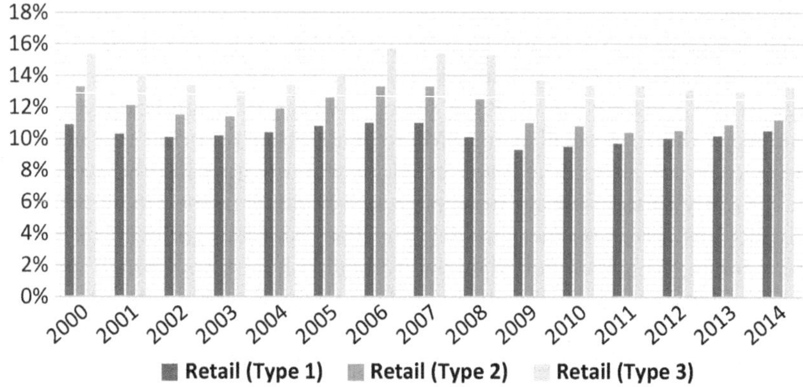

Fig. 10.5 Net worth ratio of credit unions. Source: Reproduced from Ayadi et al. (2017). Note: The net worth ratios in this are the assets-weighted means of the individual net worth ratios

15-year period covered, followed by retail type 2 and retail type 1 credit unions respectively. All in all, average net worth was more than sufficient for credit unions to be considered well capitalised, assuming they are not complex.

10.4 Regulation and Business Models in Canada

The regulatory capital ratios suggest that the retail-oriented banks respond with significantly higher average risk weights than investment banks. The latter exhibits significantly higher Tier 1 ratios thanks to relatively lower RWAs. Investment banks respond with higher (tangible common) equity and the diversified retail banks with the lowest levels (below the average values).

Among the ownership structures, the average risk weights are close to the sample median, the lowest exhibited by the diversified retail business model and the highest by the foreign banks. Overall, the domestic banks have the weakest capital position and the foreign banks exhibits the highest tangible common equity as a percentage of total assets—which can reflect on their relatively lower leveraging position as compared to the others.

The liquidity ratios of the retail business models are significantly higher than the investment models. Across ownership structures domestic banks and credit unions have a more comfortable liquidity position than the foreign counterparts, which are below average value of the sector (Table 10.7).

Table 10.7 Regulatory and supervisory indicators in Canada

(a) Business models

	Diversified retail	*Focused retail*	*Investment oriented*	*All*
Risk-weighted assets (RWA) (% of assets)	36.4%**	54.09%**	25.06%**	36.93%
Tier 1 capital ratio (% of risk-weighted assets)	12.54%*	12.69%*	36.73%**	12.66%
Total regulatory capital (% of risk-weighted assets)	15.00%*	14.72%*	36.35%**	15.09%
Tangible common equity (% tang. assets)	4.00%**	6.24%*	9.62%*	4.14%
NSFR (Avail./req. funding)	116.3%*	113.1%*	108.58%	116.11%

(b) Ownership structure

	Local banks and Desjardins group	*Foreign banks*	*Credit unions*	*All*
Risk-weighted assets (RWA) (% of assets)	36.31%	50.94%	43.70%	36.93%
Tier 1 capital ratio (% of risk-weighted assets)	12.44%	16.44%	14.73%	12.66%
Total regulatory capital (% of risk-weighted assets)	14.93%	18.44%	15.11%	15.09%
Tangible common equity (% tang. assets)	3.97%	7.04%	6.12%	4.14%
NSFR (Avail./req. funding)	116.35%	108.87%	116.12%	116.11%

Source: Author

Notes: All figures are the weighted averages values for the relevant sub-sample. The independence of clusters was tested using non-parametric equality-of-weighted averages two-sample tests at 5% significance. According to the results of these tests, the number of asterisks (*, ** or ***) stands for the statistical difference of any given cluster/ownership structure from that number of other clusters/ownership structures for that indicator. For example, two asterisks (**) imply that the cluster is statistically different from two (furthest) clusters but not the third (closest) one. See Appendix G for the assumptions pertaining to the construction of the net stable funding ratio (NSFR) measure

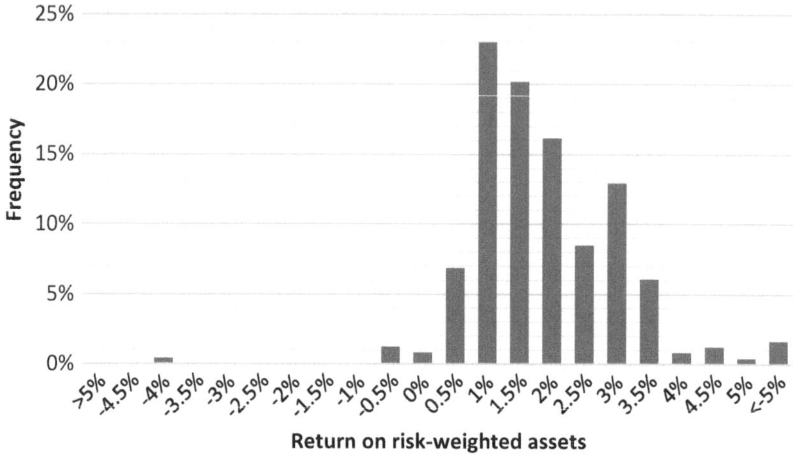

Fig. 10.6 Distribution of risk-weighted returns (RoRWA) in Canada. Source: Author

To assess the resilience of business models under stress event, Fig. 10.6 provides an illustration of the distribution of the risk-weighted returns for all banks and years in the sample. The highest frequency of the distribution is around 1% RoRWA, implying healthy returns for most banks in normal years. Assuming that a bad year is defined as a once-in-a-10-year event, that is, lower 10th and 5th percentiles losses, banks face no losses (see Figs. 10.6 and 10.7). If a bad year is defined to be a rarer and, thus, a more destructive event, that is, lower 1st percentile, the potential losses increase to maximum 1%. However, the potential losses increase faced by diversified and focused retail banks and similarly by foreign banks are much higher than the average of 1% faced by all banks.

To conclude, the response of bank business models to regulatory metrics and stress conditions simulation shows that business models matter. Generally, retail-oriented banks seem more resilient than investment and wholesale banks. There is certainly more work to be done to calibrate the one-size-fits-all regulatory approach to business models of banks.

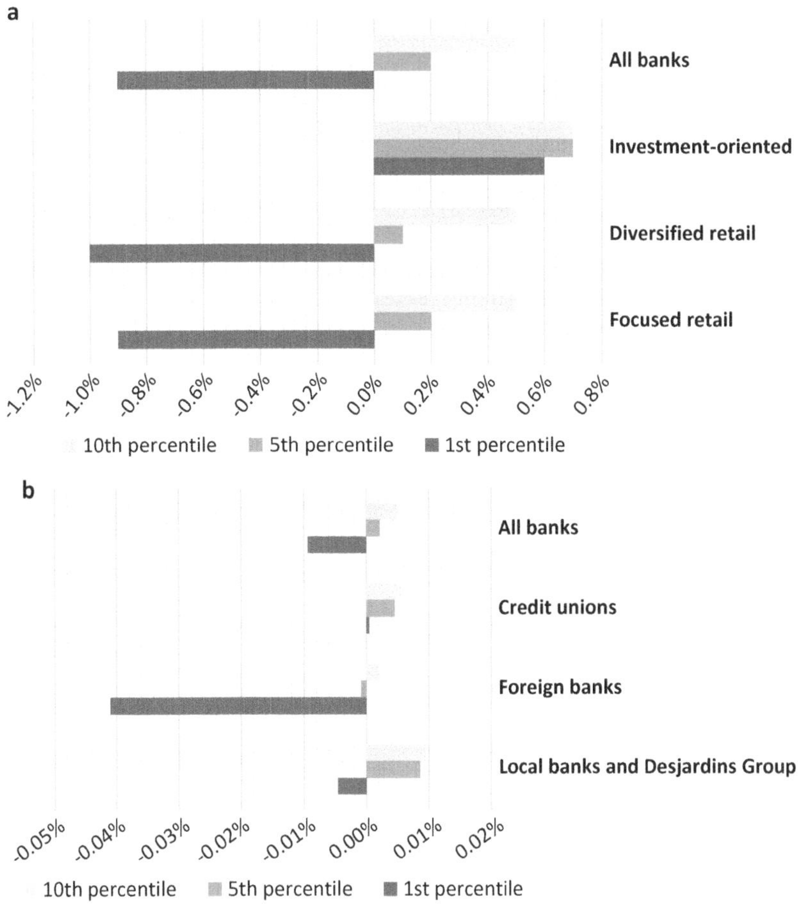

Fig. 10.7 Return on risk-weighted assets (top percentiles) in Canada. (**a**) Business models (**b**) Ownership structures. Source: Author

REFERENCES

Ayadi, R. and A. Resti (2004), The New Basel capital accord and the future of the European financial system, CEPS Taskforce Report, 51, CEPS, Brussels.

Ayadi, R. and W.P. de Groen (2014), "Banking Business Models Monitor 2014: Europe", Montreal, Joint Centre for European Policy Studies (CEPS) and International Observatory on Financial Service Cooperatives (IOFSC) publication (http://www.ceps.eu/book/banking-business-modelsmonitor-2014-europe).

Ayadi, R., E. Arbak and W.P. de Groen (2011), *Business Models in European Banking: A pre-and post-crisis screening*, Centre for European Policy Studies (CEPS), Brussels.

Ayadi, R., E. Arbak and W.P. de Groen (2012), *Regulation of European Banks and Business Models: Towards a new paradigm?*, Centre for European Policy Studies (CEPS), Brussels.

Ayadi, R. et al. (2016a), "Banking Business Models Monitor 2015: Europe", Montreal, International Research Centre on Cooperative Finance, HEC Montreal.

Ayadi, R. et al. (2017), "Bank and Credit Unions Business Models in the United States", Montreal, International Research Centre on Cooperative Finance, HEC Montreal.

Ayadi, R., Ferri, G. and V. Pesic (2016b), "Regulatory Arbitrage in EU Banking: Do Business Models Matter?" Montreal, International Research Centre on Cooperative Finance (IRCCF) Working paper.

BCBS (2010), "Calibrating regulatory minimum capital requirements and capital buffers: A top-down approach", Basel Committee on Banking Supervision, Bank for International Settlements, Basel, October.

BCBS (2013), "Regulatory Consistency Assessment Programme (RCAP): Analysis of risk-weighted assets for credit risk in the banking book", Bank for International Settlements, July.

Das, S. and A.N.R. Sy (2012), "How Risky Are Banks' Risk Weighted Assets? Evidence from the Financial Crisis", IMF Working Paper No. WP/12/36, International Monetary Fund (IMF), Washington, DC.

Harrell, F.E. and C.E. Davis (1982), "A new distribution-free quantile estimator", *Biometrika*, Vol. 69, No. 3, pp. 635–640.

CHAPTER 11

Resolution and Business Models

In Europe, policy responses to the great financial crisis have emphasised the completion of Banking Union—mainly the resolution pillar enacted under the European legislative framework known as the **Bank Recovery and Resolution Directive** (BRRD).

Depending on their business model, ownership structure and size, banks respond differently to these resolution metrics that are not calibrated to the business models. The feasibility and the credibility of their response are essential for the **stability and safety of the financial system**.

This chapter exposes the resolutions indicators used and shows the results of how business models of banks in Europe respond to the resolution requirements. The same exercise can be done for US and Canadian banks,[1] but the results are not illustrated in this chapter.

11.1 Resolution Indicators

To implement the BRRD, in July 2015 the European Banking Authority (EBA) released the Regulatory Technical Standards (RTS) for determining the **Minimum Requirement Eligible Liability** (MREL) for credit institutions in the European Economic Area (EEA). The Minimum

[1] Ongoing research by the author.

R. Ayadi, *Banking Business Models*, Palgrave Macmillan Studies in Banking and Financial Institutions,
https://doi.org/10.1007/978-3-030-02248-8_11

Requirement Eligible Liability is the minimum loss absorption requirement on a going-concern basis. To comply with it, banks in Europe must issue enough bail-inable liabilities to allow a smooth resolution with the least possible reliance on taxpayers' money or the resolution fund. As it applies to all institutions, the scope of MREL is broader than that of **Total Loss Absorption Capacity (TLAC)** standards, which applies only to the **Globally Systemic Important Banks** (GSIBs).

The TLAC approach proposed by the international standards setters[2] is close to the capital buffer approach, while the European MREL approach combines both capital buffers and incentives. The buffer approach is rooted in the view of risk as an exogenous factor, while the incentive approach acknowledges moral hazard issues in bank management and considers risk as an endogenous choice.

We should emphasise there are various similarities in the bail-in instruments allowed in each framework. Not surprisingly, both frameworks endorse the eligibility of the various capital instruments defined by the Basel agreements—subordinated debt, fixed term and corporate deposits and financial sector liabilities maturing after more than one year. A number of liabilities are excluded from bail-in. These are deposit guarantee scheme covered deposits, retail deposits of small and medium Enterprises, short-term corporate deposits, covered bonds, mortgage bonds, securitised liabilities, liabilities from repurchase agreement transactions, liabilities arising from derivatives, liabilities to employees and tax authorities, fiduciary liabilities and liabilities related to maintaining critical services at a bank under resolution.

To estimate the MREL, Ayadi and Ferri (2016) implement a two-step procedure following: First, they use the TLAC formula; and then they complement the analysis by shock simulations to assess the resilience of European banks in extreme stress conditions. These are necessary in order to provide a view as to whether the MREL requirements are sufficient.

[2] It should also be remembered that BCBS and FSB have no legislative powers and only foster international cooperation. Their aim is, therefore, to set minimum international standards and leave discretionary rulemaking to the regulatory authorities of participating countries. It is no coincidence that Europe's MREL legislation includes more discretionary tools for supervision authorities than FSB's proposal for TLAC.

11.1.1 Computation of MREL Using the TLAC Formula

From the Financial Stability Board (FSB) term sheet, a formula for the TLAC according to the requirements of 2022 can be cast as: TLAC = Max (18% RWA, 6.75% LRE), where LRE is the leverage ratio exposure. It is the denominator of the leverage ratio as per Basel III. The leverage ratio exposure of the Basel III agreement is the sum of total assets on the balance sheet and a number of (potentially substantial) off-balance sheet adjustments. It is important to note that the leverage ratio framework is not yet implemented in most European countries, and the LRE is estimated in our study by subtracting intangible assets from total assets. The estimations are done separately for component 1 and component 2 of the formulae.

11.1.2 Simulation of Shocks

In this method, the loss absorption amount is calibrated according to the peak losses over the ten-year period covered by the database (see Ayadi et al. 2016; BCBS 2010). It can be argued that, during this period, peak losses have been particularly high because of the worst financial crisis in a century. However, because of the bailouts enjoyed by the European financial system, the true picture of potential losses is probably worse than the results reported below. Thus, a calibration can use the 1st percentile plus an add-on of 2–4 percentage points to set a requirement for the loss absorption amount.

11.1.3 MREL Gap

Ayadi and Ferri (2016) defined a measure of the MREL gap as follows:

$$\text{MREL Gap} = \text{MREL} - \text{Capital}$$

In the previous expression, capital, like MREL, is expressed as a percentage of liabilities and own funds.

11.2 Resolution and Business Models in Europe

11.2.1 MREL by Bank Business Model

We assume that the MREL is computed based on the TLAC standard applied to the entire banking sector in Europe to show to what extent the business models matter. The computation uses the formula max (18% RWA, 6.75% LRE) as a percentage of total liability and own funds.

Table 11.1 MREL estimations by business models for all banks, unweighted

Business models	*18% RWAs*			*6.75% LRE*			*Max (18% RWA, 6.75% LRE)*		
	No. Obs	*Mean (%)*	*Median (%)*	*No. Obs*	*Mean (%)*	*Median (%)*	*No. Obs*	*Mean (%)*	*Median (%)*
Focused retail	2263	11.63	11.43	2301	6.64	6.64	2263	11.71	11.43
Diversified retail type 1	3759	10.30	10.00	3780	6.60	6.59	3759	10.35	10.00
Diversified retail type 2	324	7.78	7.15	336	6.66	6.74	324	8.96	7.15
Wholesale	720	7.64	7.03	731	6.69	6.71	720	8.43	7.04
Investment	1848	10.72	11.21	1853	6.69	6.70	1848	11.07	11.21
Total	8914	10.42	10.33	9001	6.64	6.64	8914	10.64	10.33

Source: Reproduced from Ayadi and Ferri (2016)

The results are reported for the first component (18% RWA) and for the second component (6.75% LRE) and for the max between the two. All results are reported unweighted. This method compares the calculations of the MREL requirements using the RWA, the LRE and the max of the two.

As displayed in Table 11.1, using the RWA formula, focused retail and investment banks have the highest requirements, followed by the diversified retail type 1. In contrast, diversified retail type 2 and wholesale banks have the lowest requirements, the mean and median of which are between 7% and 8%. Based on the LRE, mean and median requirements converge to values slightly lower than 6.75% for all business models. Thus, the LRE-based requirements do not backstop those based on RWA since the latter are much higher. The combined requirements based on RWA and LRE confirm these comments.

As for Domestically Systemic Important Banks (DSIBs) and based on the RWA (Table 11.2), the median and mean requirements are strikingly low (in the range of 4.3% to 5.4%) for diversified retail type 2 banks and wholesale banks, compared to the industry (9.23%). As a consequence, the LRE-based requirements, which are slightly lower than 6.75%, are binding for most banks in these business models, and the combined maximum requirements reflect this situation. Interestingly, the median requirement for DSIBs is not affected by the backstop of the LRE requirement which is an indication that the LRE-based requirement has indeed only affected the lowest requirements of banks in these two business models, which are also the least populated.

Table 11.2 MREL estimations by business models for DSIBs, unweighted

Business models	*18% RWAs*			*6.75% LRE*			*Max (18% RWA, 6.75% LRE)*		
	No. Obs	*Mean (%)*	*Median (%)*	*No. Obs*	*Mean (%)*	*Median (%)*	*No. Obs*	*Mean (%)*	*Median (%)*
Focused retail	79	11.64	12.04	79	6.67	6.67	79	11.68	12.04
Diversified retail type 1	142	9.37	9.76	142	6.66	6.67	142	9.66	9.76
Diversified retail type 2	32	5.25	4.32	32	6.72	6.72	32	7.21	6.74
Wholesale	67	5.35	4.52	67	6.72	6.73	67	7.13	6.76
Investment	327	9.08	9.17	327	6.65	6.64	327	9.84	9.17
Total	647	8.88	9.23	647	6.67	6.67	647	9.61	9.23

Source: Reproduced from Ayadi and Ferri (2016)

Table 11.3 MREL estimations by ownership structure for all banks, unweighted

Ownership structure	*18% RWAs*			*6.75% LRE*			*Max (18% RWA, 6.75% LRE)*		
	No. Obs	*Mean (%)*	*Median (%)*	*No. Obs*	*Mean (%)*	*Median (%)*	*No. Obs*	*Mean (%)*	*Median (%)*
Commercial	2114	10.84	10.82	2149	6.69	6.70	2114	11.21	10.82
Cooperative	4013	10.35	10.36	4053	6.62	6.62	4013	10.46	10.36
Nationalised	233	9.29	9.87	235	6.64	6.64	233	10.04	9.87
Public	179	7.63	5.69	181	6.70	6.71	179	9.36	6.77
Savings	2375	10.48	10.17	2383	6.62	6.62	2375	10.59	10.17
Total	8914	10.42	10.33	9001	6.64	6.64	8914	10.64	10.33

Source: Reproduced from Ayadi and Ferri (2016)

11.2.2 *MREL by Ownership Structure*

As regards to ownership structures (Table 11.3), median requirements based on RWA are particularly low for public banks. The LRE-based requirements slightly correct for that low median level, pushing it from 5.69% to 6.77% in the combined maximum requirements. As well, mean requirements for nationalised banks noticeably increase between their RWA estimate and the combined RWA and LRE maximum requirements.

Table 11.4 MREL gap by business model as a percentage of liabilities and own funds, unweighted

Business model	*No. Obs*	*Mean total capital (%)*	*TLAC*	
			Mean gap (%)	*Mean MREL (%)*
Focused retail	79	7.45	4.23	11.68
Diversified retail type 1	169	6.98	2.54	9.52
Diversified retail type 2	32	4.05	3.16	7.21
Wholesale	129	4.20	2.81	7.01
Investment	372	6.20	3.42	9.62
All	781	6.08	3.20	9.28

Source: Reproduced from Ayadi and Ferri (2016)

11.2.3 *Estimation of MREL by Bank Business Model*

Table 11.4 reports the mean gap for each business model as a measure of the stress to comply for systemically important banks.[3] Like the MREL, total capital is expressed as a percentage of liabilities and own funds.

Instead of the median usually reported so far, the mean gap is reported because of its linearity. It allows to directly check the relation:

$$\text{Mean Total capital} + \text{Mean MREL Gap} = \text{Mean MREL}$$

Most banks experience a gap to comply to the MREL using the TLAC method. The diversified retail type 1 banks are among the least affected while focused retail banks are more affected.

Table 11.5 reports the same indicators by ownership structure. It shows that the mean gap or stress to comply for the nationalised banks is the highest as compared to the other forms of ownerships.

[3]For non-systemic banks, the gap is a surplus (negative gap) for more than 90% of the observations.

Table 11.5 MREL gap by ownership structure as a percentage of liabilities and own funds, unweighted

Ownership structure	*No. Obs*	*Mean total capital (%)*	*TLAC*	
			Mean gap (%)	*Mean MREL (%)*
Commercial	249	6.34	3.01	9.35
Cooperative	195	6.48	3.46	9.94
Nationalised	155	5.85	3.55	9.40
Public	51	4.37	2.97	7.64
Savings	131	5.80	2.88	8.68
All	781	6.08	3.20	9.28

Source: Reproduced from Ayadi and Ferri (2016)

Table 11.6 Profit/loss by business model as a percentage of liabilities and own funds, unweighted

Business model	*No. Obs*	*Mean (%)*	*Median (%)*	*1st perc. (%)*	*5th perc. (%)*	*10th perc. (%)*
Focused retail	2301	0.52	0.53	−3.83	−1.04	0.03
Diversified retail type 1	3777	0.46	0.49	−3.33	−0.29	0.13
Diversified retail type 2	336	0.24	0.39	−24.23	−2.20	−0.18
Wholesale	729	0.53	0.45	−7.92	−1.50	−0.36
Investment	1852	0.30	0.38	−3.58	−1.20	−0.42
Total	8995	0.44	0.48	−4.14	−0.89	0.01

Source: Reproduced from Ayadi and Ferri (2016)

11.2.4 *Shock Simulations*

The results displayed by bank business model (Table 11.6) suggest that under an extreme stress condition, such as the events experienced in the financial crisis 2007–2008, on average, 4.15% losses as a percentage of liabilities and own funds are wiped out from the banking system. Hence, this result suggests a minimum loss absorption requirement of at least 4.15% for all banks. An additional requirement of up to 20% can be imposed on diversified retail type 2, so that it can cover the above average

Table 11.7 Profit/loss by ownership structure as a percentage of liabilities and own funds, unweighted

Ownership structure	*No. Obs*	*Mean (%)*	*Median (%)*	*1st perc. (%)*	*5th perc. (%)*	*10th perc. (%)*
Commercial	2145	0.48	0.61	−7.48	−2.36	−0.86
Cooperative	4053	0.45	0.48	−2.16	−0.24	0.13
Nationalised	235	−0.60	0.11	−13.08	−6.64	−2.62
Public	181	−0.11	0.27	−6.41	−1.97	−0.10
Savings	2381	0.53	0.46	−2.14	−0.07	0.11
Total	8995	0.44	0.48	−4.14	−0.89	0.01

Source: Reproduced from Ayadi and Ferri (2016)

additional losses as a percentage of their liability and own funds. Similarly, wholesale banks would incur an additional requirement of up to 3.75%, to account for the riskiness of their business models compared to the average bank. These results suggest that the MREL parameters may undergo serious tail risk for diversified retail type 2 banks and also, to a lesser extent, for wholesale banks.

Similarly, the results per bank ownership structure (Table 11.7) suggest a penalty of up to 8.9% can be imposed on nationalised banks so that their requirement will cover the more than 13% of losses as a percentage of their liability and own funds. Similarly, commercial banks would incur a penalty of about 3.3% to account for the particular riskiness of their ownership structure, while public banks will face an additional 2.25% of MREL requirement.

Of course, the regulator would apply some combination of the penalty formulae to account simultaneously for the business model and the ownership structure.

Peak losses at the 1st percentile seem to really discriminate among the three systemic groups. Up to a 3.9% penalty should be imposed to DSIB on top of the basic requirement of 4.15%, so as to cover 8.05% potential losses in case of distress.

It is important to notice that the real picture is somewhat blurred because of the bailouts of EU banks since the beginning of the financial crisis. Without any bailouts, the losses results would have been much higher than reported in these estimations, especially for the GSIBs (Table 11.8).

Table 11.8 Profit/loss by systemic group as a percentage of liabilities and own funds, unweighted

Systemic group	*No. Obs*	*Mean (%)*	*Median (%)*	*1st perc. (%)*	*5th perc. (%)*	*10th perc. (%)*
GSIB	132	0.50	0.51	−1.84	−0.37	−0.04
DSIB	646	0.12	0.33	−8.05	−1.84	−0.80
NSB	8217	0.47	0.48	−3.89	−0.79	0.04
Total	8995	0.44	0.48	−4.14	−0.89	0.01

Source: Reproduced from Ayadi and Ferri (2016)

Note: NSB – non systemic banks

To conclude, all business models exhibit a gap to comply to MREL calibrated to TLAC, but there is a difference between business models. Therefore, the one-size-fits-all resolution approach applied in Europe might be miscalibrated and that would be detrimental to the overall recovery of the financial system.

References

Ayadi, R and G. Ferri (2016), Total Assets versus RWA: does it matter for MREL requirements, European Parliament, Brussels.

Ayadi, R. et al. (2016), "Banking Business Models Monitor 2015: Europe", Montreal, International Research Centre On Cooperative Finance, HEC Montreal.

BCBS (2010), "Calibrating regulatory minimum capital requirements and capital buffers: A top-down approach", Basel Committee on Banking Supervision, Bank for International Settlements, Basel, October.

CHAPTER 12

Conclusions

This book reviews the reasons and the process, describes the datasets, and exposes the methodology, computations and analysis used to develop the BBM analysis framework. It explains the relevance of this new **framework for financial stability assessment and future of regulation and resolution**.

It provided an overview on the evolving role of banks in **the financial system**—with a focus on why banks changed their business model over the past decades and how the literature explained it using the diversification benefits from the assets and liability sides.

It proposed a novel definition of a bank business model emphasising the activities on the asset side and the funding on the liability side. This new definition provides a holistic view as to how a bank behaves in the market while transforming its funding (retail, market or mixed) into retail, market or both financing and investment opportunities. The definition allows comparability between countries and all types of banks (and credit unions when data is available).

It identified the business models banks for comprehensive large datasets of banks and credit unions (when data is available) in Europe, US and Canada using the clustering methodology that is a simple data-driven statistical technique for assigning a set of observations into distinct group.

R. Ayadi, *Banking Business Models*, Palgrave Macmillan Studies in Banking and Financial Institutions,
https://doi.org/10.1007/978-3-030-02248-8_12

The results of the computations to identify business models in Europe, US and Canada show that:

- In Europe, there are five bank business models which include three retail oriented with different levels of activity diversification and funding mix and one investment and another wholesale oriented;
- In the US, there are four bank business models which include two types of retail oriented, one investment and another wholesale and three types of retail-oriented credit unions with different levels of activity and funding;
- In Canada, there are three business models, which include two retail oriented with different level of diversification and one investment.

These broad categories hide important distinctions within each business model that could be explored by further research.

It explained how the business models analysis could form part of the financial stability assessment framework and serve as a policy tool in terms of prevention, remedy and resolution. The business model assessment framework was performed and included: how business models interact with the other traditional metrics such as size and ownership and organisational structure, the determinants of business models migration and contribution to systemic risk, how business models contribute to financial and economic performance, how they increase and manage risks and how they respond to regulation and resolution.

The analysis shows:

- Crossing business models in banks with size and ownership and organisational structure show that business models analysis adds a new analytical dimension to better understand the architecture of the banking system and to contribute to financial stability assessment and stability.
- The migration analysis shows a generally low percentage of business models migration between business models. This phenomenon should be better researched to better understand the reasons and impacts of migration (in general and the direction of the migration), the process of accumulation and dissipation of risk in the system during the process of migration and to assess whether migration leads to financial stability or instability.

- The performance and risk analysis shows a difference in performance and risk between different business models during the economic cycle in all countries surveyed. Generally, investment-oriented banks are performing financially while accumulating more risk in the system as compared to the retail-oriented banks which are financial performing and allocating funding to the real economy and are generally more resilient than their counterparts to external shocks. However, the wholesale and wholesale-funded retail-oriented banks must be carefully assessed as they exhibit vulnerabilities in terms of risk related to these business models.
- The response of bank business models to regulation, supervision and resolution shows that business models matter when assessing the response to all regulatory metrics. There is certainly more work to be done to calibrate the one-size-fits-all regulatory and resolution approach to business models of banks.

The business model analysis has a predictive power that is essential for regulators and supervisors to detect excessive risk accumulation at a system level over a period of time and, especially, when external shocks are simulated. Moreover, understanding the systemic risk accumulation process is paramount to achieving a targeted macro-prudential regulation in close cooperation with active micro-prudential regulation and supervision. Grouping into a business model those institutions that have a tendency to drive systemic risk upward, and acting accordingly with the appropriate regulatory and supervisory measures, would be the beginning of a new dynamic and targeted regulatory and supervisory framework. This would complement the current framework, which when improved would work together in tandem to prevent massive bank failures.

If prevention fails, resolution must, at least, be well designed to ensure an orderly resolution and liquidation, without putting taxpayers in line to save banks, as was done to deal with the GFC. Calibrating the MREL and also the TLAC to business models is essential to ensure that, in the resolution phase, there is no miscalibration that would be largely detrimental to the overall recovery of the financial system.

Importantly, transparency and public disclosure practices remain an important concern. The disclosure practices of banks, which are of fundamental importance to cross-border banking review and comparison, remain largely incomplete and incomparable. Issues relate to differences in definitions, limited disclosure particularly of banks that are not listed in Europe and Canada.

Finally, further research on financial institutions business models should explore other definitions, other methodologies to identify the business models and better understand how bank (and other financial institutions) business models can be a policy tool and an indicator to explain and assess systemic risk accumulation and financial stability and un-stability and whether or not it is desirable to a diverse financial system or on the contrary one single "healthy" business model for better intermediating savings to productive investment opportunities in the economy.

Correction to: Banking Business Models

CORRECTION TO:

R. Ayadi, *Banking Business Models*, Palgrave Macmillan Studies in Banking and Financial Institutions, https://doi.org/10.1007/978-3-030-02248-8

Owing to an oversight, Appendix A was originally published incompletely. The complete version is presented here:

The updated version of the book can be found at https://doi.org/10.1007/978-3-030-02248-8

R. Ayadi, *Banking Business Models*, Palgrave Macmillan Studies in Banking and Financial Institutions,
https://doi.org/10.1007/978-3-030-02248-8_13

No.	Variable	Coverage	No.	Variable	Coverage
1	Country (headquarter location)	100%	32	Share price (daily return)	67%
2	Reporting currency	100%	33	Share price (st. dev. daily return)	67%
3	Accounting method	100%	34	Share price (market Beta)	67%
4	Annual report (pages)	100%	35	Share price (interest Beta)	67%
5	Accounting date (end of year)	100%	36	Employees (FTEs)	65%
6	Annual report (approval date)	96%	37	Employees (FTEs—Male)	21%
7	Accounting firm	100%	38	Employees (FTEs—Female)	21%
8	Total accounting fee	90%	39	Employees (headcount)	56%
9	Total non-audit fee	88%	40	Employees (headcount—Male)	25%
10	Ownership (SHV/STV)	100%	41	Employees (headcount—Female)	25%
11	Ownership (cooperative, savings, etc.)	100%	42	Employees (domestic)	69%
12	Public ownership (%)	100%	43	Employees (other EU27 countries)	38%
13	Public ownership (domestic %)	100%	44	Employees (outside EU27)	69%
14	Public ownership (domestic name)	31%	45	Employees (training hours)	29%
15	Public ownership (other EU27 %)	100%	46	Employees (training employees)	19%
16	Public ownership (other EU27 name)	7%	47	Branches (total)	92%
17	Public ownership (outside EU27 %)	100%	48	Branches (domestic)	83%
18	Public ownership (outside EU27 name)	8%	49	Branches (other EU27 countries)	47%
19	Largest shareholder (% ownership)	90%	50	Branches (outside EU27)	76%
20	Largest shareholder (name)	94%	51	ATMs (total)	31%
21	Block holder ownership (>5%)	87%	52	ATMs (domestic)	25%
22	Block holder ownership (>3%)	63%	53	ATMs (other EU27 countries)	14%
23	Listed (YES/NO)	100%	54	ATMs (outside EU27)	11%
24	Ordinary shares (outstanding)	72%	55	Assets (total)	100%
25	Ordinary shares (traded)	66%	56	Assets (domestic)	56%
26	Market capitalisation	72%	57	Cash (and balances with central banks)	100%
27	Value of traded shares	66%	58	Assets (central bank)	60%
28	Gross dividend	72%	59	Loans to banks (total)	100%
29	Share price (year end)	72%	60	Loans to banks (nostro accounts/on demand)	27%
30	Share price (average)	67%	61	Loans to banks (loan loss provision)	58%
31	Share price (standard deviation)	67%	62	Loans to customers (total)	96%

63	Loans to customers (public sector)	28%	94	CDS spread (subordinated, volatility)	62%
64	Loans to customers (mortgage loans)	51%	95	Income (total)	100%
65	Loans to customers (loan loss provision)	69%	96	Income (interest—net)	100%
66	Loans to customers (collective impairment)	22%	97	Income (interest—income)	94%
67	Loans to customers (specific impairment)	22%	98	Income (interest—expenses)	94%
68	Intangible assets	100%	99	Income (non-interest)	100%
69	Goodwill	100%	100	Income (commissions—net)	100%
70	Reverse repurchase agreements	89%	101	Income (commissions—income)	91%
71	Liabilities (total)	100%	102	Income (commissions—expenses)	91%
72	Liabilities (domestic)	27%	103	Income (trading—net)	98%
73	Liabilities (banks incl. central banks)	96%	104	Income (dividend)	38%
74	Deposits (banks)	72%	105	Income (insurance—net)	74%
75	Deposits (domestic banks)	27%	106	Income (insurance—income)	72%
76	Deposits (central banks)	44%	107	Income (insurance—expenses)	72%
77	Deposits (banks—demand)	46%	108	Income (other)	94%
78	Deposits (banks—term)	43%	109	Expenses (operating—total)	100%
79	Liabilities (customers)	96%	110	Expenses (operating—administrative)	99%
80	Deposits (customers)	80%	111	Expenses (operating—personal)	93%
81	Deposits (domestic customers)	42%	112	Expenses (operating—personal training)	27%
82	Deposits (customers—term and time deposits)	54%	113	Expenses (operating—other)	93%
83	Deposits (customers—current accounts and demand)	46%	114	Expenses (operating—depreciations)	99%
84	Deposits (customers—savings)	55%	115	Profit (before tax)	100%
85	Repurchase agreements (liabilities)	92%	116	Income tax	100%
86	Short-selling position (total)	63%	117	Profit (after tax)	100%
87	Short-selling position (equity)	7%	118	Risk-weighted assets (total)	87%
88	Short-selling position (debt)	7%	119	Risk-weighted assets (off balance sheet)	16%
89	CDS spread (senior, year end)	69%	120	Risk-weighted assets (credit risk)	36%
90	CDS spread (senior, average)	69%	121	Risk-weighted assets (market risk)	36%
91	CDS spread (senior, volatility)	69%	122	Risk-weighted assets (operational risk)	30%
92	CDS spread (subordinated, year end)	62%	123	Risk-weighted assets (business risk)	10%
93	CDS spread (subordinated, average)	62%	124	Capital (regulatory capital)	93%
			125	Capital (tier I—total)	93%

(*continued*)

(continued)

No.	Variable	Coverage	No.	Variable	Coverage
126	Capital (tier I—core)	27%	152	Derivatives (total—nominal value)	22%
127	Capital (tier I—hybrid)	56%	153	Derivatives (total—notional value)	55%
128	Capital (tier II—total)	76%	154	Derivatives (total—notional value—receive)	14%
129	Capital (tier II—subordinated liabilities)	27%	155	Derivatives (total—notional value—deliver)	14%
130	Capital (tier II—hybrid)	15%	156	Derivatives (total—fair value—positive)	95%
131	Capital (tier III—total)	76%	157	Derivatives (total—fair value—negative)	95%
132	Capital (equity—total)	100%	158	Derivatives (interest—nominal value)	22%
133	Capital (equity—shareholders)	100%	159	Derivatives (interest—notional value)	55%
134	Capital (equity—minority interest)	100%	160	Derivatives (interest—notional value—receive)	14%
135	Capital (equity—special securities)	100%	161	Derivatives (interest—notional value—deliver)	14%
136	Capital (equity—hybrid)	100%	162	Derivatives (interest—fair value—positive)	92%
137	Capital (equity—subordinated liabilities)	100%	163	Derivatives (interest—fair value—negative)	92%
138	Capital (equity—hybrid)	100%	164	Derivatives (currency—nominal value)	22%
139	Capital (tangible common equity)	100%	165	Derivatives (currency—notional value)	55%
140	Capital (common equity)	100%	166	Derivatives (currency—notional value—receive)	14%
141	Capital (common stock)	96%	167	Derivatives (currency—notional value—deliver)	14%
142	Capital (additional paid-in capital)	96%	168	Derivatives (currency—fair value—positive)	92%
143	Capital (retained earnings)	100%	169	Derivatives (currency—fair value—negative)	92%
144	Capital (treasury shares)	98%	170	Derivatives (equity—nominal value)	22%
145	Capital (non-recognised losses)	99%	171	Derivatives (equity—notional value)	55%
146	Capital (subscribed capital—issuance)	100%	172	Derivatives (equity—notional value—receive)	14%
147	Capital (non-common equity—issuance)	100%	173	Derivatives (equity—notional value—deliver)	14%
148	Rating (DBRS)	19%	174	Derivatives (equity—fair value—positive)	92%
149	Rating (Fitch)	69%	175	Derivatives (equity—fair value—negative)	92%
150	Rating (Moody's)	80%	176	Derivatives (credit—nominal value)	22%
151	Rating (S&P)	79%	177	Derivatives (credit—notional value)	55%
			178	Derivatives (credit—notional value—receive)	18%

179	Derivatives (credit—notional value—deliver)	18%	191	Derivatives (hedging—notional value)	30%
180	Derivatives (credit—fair value—positive)	93%	192	Derivatives (hedging—fair value—positive)	78%
181	Derivatives (credit—fair value—negative)	92%	193	Derivatives (hedging—fair value—negative)	78%
182	Derivatives (FX—nominal value)	15%	194	Derivatives (trading—notional value—receive)	11%
183	Derivatives (FX—notional value)	27%	195	Derivatives (trading—notional value—deliver)	11%
184	Derivatives (FX—fair value—positive)	37%	196	Derivatives (trading—fair value—positive)	79%
185	Derivatives (FX—fair value—negative)	37%	197	Derivatives (trading—fair value—negative)	78%
186	Derivatives (OTC—nominal value)	19%	198	Asset-backed securities (total)	34%
187	Derivatives (OTC—notional value)	22%	199	Asset-backed securities (impaired)	11%
188	Derivatives (OTC—fair value—positive)	37%	200	Asset-backed securities (CDOs)	22%
189	Derivatives (OTC—fair value—negative)	37%	201	Asset-backed securities (RMBSs)	21%
190	Derivatives (hedging—nominal value)	13%	202	Asset-backed securities (CMBSs)	19%

Appendix A: List of Indicators

R. Ayadi, *Banking Business Models*, Palgrave Macmillan Studies in Banking and Financial Institutions,
https://doi.org/10.1007/978-3-030-02248-8

No.	*Variable*	*Coverage*	*No.*	*Variable*	*Coverage*
1	Country (headquarter location)	100%	32	Share price (daily return)	67%
2	Reporting currency	100%	33	Share price (st. dev. daily return)	67%
3	Accounting method	100%	34	Share price (market Beta)	67%
4	Annual report (pages)	100%	35	Share price (interest Beta)	67%
5	Accounting date (end of year)	100%	36	Employees (FTEs)	65%
6	Annual report (approval date)	96%	37	Employees (FTEs—Male)	21%
7	Accounting firm	100%	38	Employees (FTEs—Female)	21%
8	Total accounting fee	90%	39	Employees (headcount)	56%
9	Total non-audit fee	88%	40	Employees (headcount—Male)	25%
10	Ownership (SHV/STV)	100%	41	Employees (headcount—Female)	25%
11	Ownership (cooperative, savings, etc.)	100%	42	Employees (domestic)	69%
12	Public ownership (%)	100%	43	Employees (other EU27 countries)	38%
13	Public ownership (domestic %)	100%	44	Employees (outside EU27)	69%
14	Public ownership (domestic name)	31%	45	Employees (training hours)	29%
15	Public ownership (other EU27 %)	100%	46	Employees (training employees)	19%
16	Public ownership (other EU27 name)	7%	47	Branches (total)	92%
17	Public ownership (outside EU27 %)	100%	48	Branches (domestic)	83%
18	Public ownership (outside EU27 name)	8%	49	Branches (other EU27 countries)	47%
19	Largest shareholder (% ownership)	90%	50	Branches (outside EU27)	76%
20	Largest shareholder (name)	94%	51	ATMs (total)	31%
21	Block holder ownership (>5%)	87%	52	ATMs (domestic)	25%
22	Block holder ownership (>3%)	63%	53	ATMs (other EU27 countries)	14%
23	Listed (YES/NO)	100%	54	ATMs (outside EU27)	11%
24	Ordinary shares (outstanding)	72%	55	Assets (total)	100%
25	Ordinary shares (traded)	66%	56	Assets (domestic)	56%
26	Market capitalisation	72%	57	Cash (and balances with central banks)	100%
27	Value of traded shares	66%	58	Assets (central bank)	60%
28	Gross dividend	72%	59	Loans to banks (total)	100%
29	Share price (year end)	72%	60	Loans to banks (nostro accounts/on demand)	27%
30	Share price (average)	67%	61	Loans to banks (loan loss provision)	58%
31	Share price (standard deviation)	67%	62	Loans to customers (total)	96%

63	Loans to customers (public sector)	28%	94	CDS spread (subordinated, volatility)	62%
64	Loans to customers (mortgage loans)	51%	95	Income (total)	100%
65	Loans to customers (loan loss provision)	69%	96	Income (interest—net)	100%
66	Loans to customers (collective impairment)	22%	97	Income (interest—income)	94%
67	Loans to customers (specific impairment)	22%	98	Income (interest—expenses)	94%
68	Intangible assets	100%	99	Income (non-interest)	100%
69	Goodwill	100%	100	Income (commissions—net)	100%
70	Reverse repurchase agreements	89%	101	Income (commissions—income)	91%
71	Liabilities (total)	100%	102	Income (commissions—expenses)	91%
72	Liabilities (domestic)	27%	103	Income (trading—net)	98%
73	Liabilities (banks incl. central banks)	96%	104	Income (dividend)	38%
74	Deposits (banks)	72%	105	Income (insurance—net)	74%
75	Deposits (domestic banks)	27%	106	Income (insurance—income)	72%
76	Deposits (central banks)	44%	107	Income (insurance—expenses)	72%
77	Deposits (banks—demand)	46%	108	Income (other)	94%
78	Deposits (banks—term)	43%	109	Expenses (operating—total)	100%
79	Liabilities (customers)	96%	110	Expenses (operating—administrative)	99%
80	Deposits (customers)	80%	111	Expenses (operating—personal)	93%
81	Deposits (domestic customers)	42%	112	Expenses (operating—personal training)	27%
82	Deposits (customers—term and time deposits)	54%	113	Expenses (operating—other)	93%
83	Deposits (customers—current accounts and demand)	46%	114	Expenses (operating—depreciations)	99%
84	Deposits (customers—savings)	55%	115	Profit (before tax)	100%
85	Repurchase agreements (liabilities)	92%	116	Income tax	100%
86	Short-selling position (total)	63%	117	Profit (after tax)	100%
87	Short-selling position (equity)	7%	118	Risk-weighted assets (total)	87%
88	Short-selling position (debt)	7%	119	Risk-weighted assets (off balance sheet)	16%
89	CDS spread (senior, year end)	69%	120	Risk-weighted assets (credit risk)	36%
90	CDS spread (senior, average)	69%	121	Risk-weighted assets (market risk)	36%
91	CDS spread (senior, volatility)	69%	122	Risk-weighted assets (operational risk)	30%
92	CDS spread (subordinated, year end)	62%	123	Risk-weighted assets (business risk)	10%
93	CDS spread (subordinated, average)	62%	124	Capital (regulatory capital)	93%
			125	Capital (tier I—total)	93%

(*continued*)

(continued)

No.	*Variable*	*Coverage*	*No.*	*Variable*	*Coverage*
126	Capital (tier I—core)	27%	152	Derivatives (total—nominal value)	22%
127	Capital (tier I—hybrid)	56%	153	Derivatives (total—notional value)	55%
128	Capital (tier II—total)	76%	154	Derivatives (total—notional value—receive)	14%
129	Capital (tier II—subordinated liabilities)	27%	155	Derivatives (total—notional value—deliver)	14%
130	Capital (tier II—hybrid)	15%	156	Derivatives (total—fair value—positive)	95%
131	Capital (tier III—total)	76%	157	Derivatives (total—fair value—negative)	95%
132	Capital (equity—total)	100%	158	Derivatives (interest—nominal value)	22%
133	Capital (equity—shareholders)	100%	159	Derivatives (interest—notional value)	55%
134	Capital (equity—minority interest)	100%	160	Derivatives (interest—notional value—receive)	14%
135	Capital (equity—special securities)	100%	161	Derivatives (interest—notional value—deliver)	14%
136	Capital (equity—hybrid)	100%	162	Derivatives (interest—fair value—positive)	92%
137	Capital (equity—subordinated liabilities)	100%	163	Derivatives (interest—fair value—negative)	92%
138	Capital (equity—hybrid)	100%	164	Derivatives (currency—nominal value)	22%
139	Capital (tangible common equity)	100%	165	Derivatives (currency—notional value)	55%
140	Capital (common equity)	100%	166	Derivatives (currency—notional value—receive)	14%
141	Capital (common stock)	96%	167	Derivatives (currency—notional value—deliver)	14%
142	Capital (additional paid-in capital)	96%	168	Derivatives (currency—fair value—positive)	92%
143	Capital (retained earnings)	100%	169	Derivatives (currency—fair value—negative)	92%
144	Capital (treasury shares)	98%	170	Derivatives (equity—nominal value)	22%
145	Capital (non-recognised losses)	99%	171	Derivatives (equity—notional value)	55%
146	Capital (subscribed capital—issuance)	100%	172	Derivatives (equity—notional value—receive)	14%
147	Capital (non-common equity—issuance)	100%	173	Derivatives (equity—notional value—deliver)	14%
148	Rating (DBRS)	19%	174	Derivatives (equity—fair value—positive)	92%
149	Rating (Fitch)	69%	175	Derivatives (equity—fair value—negative)	92%
150	Rating (Moody's)	80%	176	Derivatives (credit—nominal value)	22%
151	Rating (S&P)	79%	177	Derivatives (credit—notional value)	55%
			178	Derivatives (credit—notional value—receive)	18%

179	Derivatives (credit—notional value—deliver)	18%	191	Derivatives (hedging—notional value)	30%
180	Derivatives (credit—fair value—positive)	93%	192	Derivatives (hedging—fair value—positive)	78%
181	Derivatives (credit—fair value—negative)	92%	193	Derivatives (hedging—fair value—negative)	78%
182	Derivatives (FX—nominal value)	15%	194	Derivatives (trading—notional value—receive)	11%
183	Derivatives (FX—notional value)	27%	195	Derivatives (trading—notional value—deliver)	11%
184	Derivatives (FX—fair value—positive)	37%	196	Derivatives (trading—fair value—positive)	79%
185	Derivatives (FX—fair value—negative)	37%	197	Derivatives (trading—fair value—negative)	78%
186	Derivatives (OTC—nominal value)	19%	198	Asset-backed securities (total)	34%
187	Derivatives (OTC—notional value)	22%	199	Asset-backed securities (impaired)	11%
188	Derivatives (OTC—fair value—positive)	37%	200	Asset-backed securities (CDOs)	22%
189	Derivatives (OTC—fair value—negative)	37%	201	Asset-backed securities (RMBSs)	21%
190	Derivatives (hedging—nominal value)	13%	202	Asset-backed securities (CMBSs)	19%

Appendix B: List of Countries in Europe

R. Ayadi, *Banking Business Models*, Palgrave Macmillan Studies in Banking and Financial Institutions,
https://doi.org/10.1007/978-3-030-02248-8

	Economic area		*Country*	*Number of institutions*	*Assets (€ billion)*
European Economic Area (EEA) 32 countries 2542 institutions €44,805 bn in assets	European Union (EU) 28 countries 2193 institutions €41,366 bn in assets	Eurozone 19 countries 1859 institutions €29,126 bn in assets	Austria	79	770.6
			Belgium	23	909.8
			Cyprus	8	127.2
			Estonia	2	0.4
			Finland	10	135.7
			France	79	7831.7
			Germany	1108	7309.5
			Greece	16	442
			Ireland	15	409.6
			Italy	314	2970.4
			Latvia	13	17.6
			Lithuania	5	5.6
			Luxembourg	33	276.7
			Malta	7	16.3
			Netherlands	30	2782.8
			Portugal	22	445.1
			Slovakia	4	9.2
			Slovenia	11	25.9
			Spain	80	4639.5
		Non-Eurozone 9 countries 334 institutions €12,241 bn in assets	Bulgaria	9	11.6
			Croatia	15	9.5
			Czech Republic	12	25.4
			Denmark	76	851.4
			Hungary	8	49.9
			Poland	13	136.1
			Romania	8	18.9
			Sweden	58	1669.6
			United Kingdom	135	9468.3
	European Free Trade Association (EFTA) 4 countries 349 institutions €3439 bn in assets		Iceland	7	25.1
			Liechtenstein	7	40.9
			Norway	90	548.7
			Switzerland	245	2824.6

Note: Assets values refer to the last available year for each institution

Appendix C: Descriptive Statistics for BBM Identification

R. Ayadi, *Banking Business Models*, Palgrave Macmillan Studies in Banking and Financial Institutions,
https://doi.org/10.1007/978-3-030-02248-8

Table C.1 Descriptive statistics for business models banks in Europe

		Bank loans (% assets)	*Customer loans (% assets)*	*Trading assets (% assets)*	*Bank liabilities (% assets)*	*Customer deposits (% assets)*	*Debt liabilities (% assets)*	*Derivative exposures (% assets)*	*Tang. Comm. eq. (% tang. assets)*
Model 1—Focused retail	Mean	7.0%	78.5%	11.8%	12.3%	69.5%	10.1%	0.3%	7.6%
	Std dev.	0.057***	0.079***	0.071***	0.141**	0.153***	0.078***	0.008***	0.054***
	Min.	0.0%	54.9%	0.1%	0.0%	0.0%	0.1%	0.0%	−6.4%
	Max.	40.2%	99.2%	27.8%	92.3%	98.3%	34.5%	16.0%	95.5%
	Obs	3877	3877	3877	3877	3877	3877	3877	3877
Model 2—Diversified retail (type 1)	Mean	10.3%	55.6%	30.9%	14.0%	70.7%	7.3%	0.4%	7.5%
	Std dev.	0.073***	0.083***	0.087***	0.11**	0.142***	0.062***	0.015***	0.057***
	Min.	0.0%	14.4%	0.0%	0.0%	0.0%	0.0%	0.0%	−6.0%
	Max.	38.8%	71.4%	54.3%	89.3%	94.6%	34.4%	20.9%	96.7%
	Obs	5048	5048	5048	5048	5048	5048	5048	4982
Model 3—Diversified retail (type 2)	Mean	6.6%	68.9%	22.6%	10.6%	36.7%	43.3%	1.7%	7.4%
	Std dev.	0.061***	0.117***	0.099***	0.088**	0.165***	0.155***	0.031***	0.045***
	Min.	0.0%	31.2%	0.1%	0.0%	0.0%	22.9%	0.0%	−12.9%
	Max.	56.4%	97.2%	57.0%	59.8%	70.1%	99.3%	24.1%	68.8%
	Obs	2023	2023	2023	2023	2023	2023	2023	1964
Model 4—Wholesale	Mean	52.2%	20.7%	17.1%	22.4%	51.8%	10.4%	0.8%	14.1%
	Std dev.	0.201***	0.151***	0.126***	0.265**	0.321***	0.193***	0.026***	0.152***
	Min.	0.0%	0.0%	0.0%	0.0%	0.0%	0.0%	0.0%	0.2%
	Max.	100.0%	55.7%	52.7%	98.1%	97.5%	99.8%	38.4%	100.0%
	Obs	887	887	887	887	887	887	887	873

Model 5—Investment	Mean	11.4%	23.5%	60.2%	14.9%	49.3%	19.9%	5.2%	9.8%
	Std dev.	0.092***	0.133***	0.158***	0.189**	0.311***	0.214***	0.125***	0.137***
	Min.	0.0%	0.0%	21.2%	0.0%	0.0%	0.0%	0.0%	−0.4%
	Max.	40.9%	48.0%	100.0%	97.7%	97.3%	100.0%	90.8%	99.9%
	Obs	1205	1205	1205	1205	1205	1205	1205	1184
All banks	Mean	11.7%	59.1%	25.7%	13.6%	61.8%	15.1%	1.0%	8.2%
	Std dev.	0.139***	0.212***	0.167***	0.143**	0.227***	0.172***	0.044***	0.078***
	Min.	0.0%	0.0%	0.0%	0.0%	0.0%	0.0%	0.0%	−12.9%
	Max.	100.0%	99.2%	100.0%	98.1%	98.3%	100.0%	90.8%	100.0%
	Obs	13,040	13,040	13,040	13,040	13,040	13,040	13,040	12,850

Source: Reproduced from Ayadi et al. (2016)

Notes: The independence of clusters was tested using non-parametric Wilcoxon-Mann-Witney two-sample tests at 5% significance. According to the results of these tests, the number of asterisks (*, **, ***, and ****) stands for the statistical difference of any given cluster from that number of other clusters for that indicator. For example, two asterisks (**) implies that the cluster is statistically different from two other clusters but not the third and fourth (closest) ones

Table C.2 Descriptive statistics for business models in banks in the US, weighted

		Loans to banks (% assets)	*Customer loans (% assets)*	*Trading assets (% assets)*	*Bank liabilities (% assets)*	*Customer deposits (% assets)*	*Debt liabilities (% assets)*	*Derivative exposures (% assets)*	*Tang. Comm. eq. (% tang. assets)*	*Cash (% assets)*
Model 1—Wholesale oriented	Median	1.44%	35.85%	34.12%	0.65%	32.71%	8.42%	5.83%	5.57%	18.55%
	Mean	2.12%***	37.3%***	33.44%***	1.06%	30.21%***	10.85%**	6.73%***	7.31%***	20.34%***
	Std dev.	2.68%	16.38%	10.48%	3.95%	11.35%	11.79%	5.32%	4.96%	11.40%
	P1.	0.00%	3.51%	0.00%	0.00%	0.00%	0.25%	0.00%	4.39%	0.51%
	P99.	12.79%	93.55%	63.77%	7.89%	47.14%	74.06%	23.77%	20.96%	52.45%
	Obs.	2665	2665	2665	2665	2665	2665	2665	2665	2665
Model 2—Retail (type 1)	Median	0.24%	55.35%	26.15%	0.71%	68.77%	6.38%	0.99%	7.12%	8.75%
	Mean	1.07%***	55.27%***	26.08%***	0.95%**	67.72%***	7.06%***	1.65%***	7.6%***	9%***
	Std dev.	2.12%	6.14%	5.40%	1.27%	11.60%	5.05%	1.94%	2.27%	6.28%
	P1.	0.00%	41.30%	10.92%	0.00%	43.89%	0.00%	0.00%	3.57%	1.12%
	P99.	11.84%	67.11%	39.80%	5.65%	90.68%	26.52%	7.38%	15.67%	33.47%
	Obs.	41,993	41,993	41,993	41,993	41,993	41,993	41,993	41,993	41,993
Model 3—Retail (type 2)	Median	0.00%	70.58%	14.79%	0.29%	69.51%	8.91%	0.04%	8.15%	4.88%
	Mean	0.56%***	71.38%***	13.57%***	1.04%**	68.33%***	10.67%**	0.44%***	8.32%**	6.24%***
	Std dev.	2.40%	7.08%	5.75%	2.82%	13.71%	9.18%	0.93%	2.94%	5.18%
	P1.	0.00%	56.93%	0.01%	0.00%	28.19%	0.00%	0.00%	2.99%	0.65%
	P99.	10.59%	90.02%	23.00%	13.82%	90.66%	40.85%	6.66%	17.51%	28.98%
	Obs.	48,739	48,739	48,739	48,739	48,739	48,739	48,739	48,739	48,739
Model 4—Investment oriented	Median	0.30%	31.22%	42.54%	0.39%	61.54%	5.82%	0.58%	7.19%	12.62%
	Mean	0.7%***	32.62%***	44.26%***	1.11%**	66.93%***	5.55%***	2.64%***	8.31%**	17.07%***
	Std dev.	1.21%	10.68%	14.83%	1.60%	16.14%	5.84%	2.94%	3.37%	13.78%
	P1.	0.00%	0.17%	21.17%	0.00%	43.85%	0.00%	0.00%	4.20%	0.07%
	P99.	5.23%	49.90%	92.65%	4.19%	93.15%	29.33%	9.60%	19.87%	51.35%
	Obs.	14,829	14,829	14,829	14,829	14,829	14,829	14,829	14,829	14,829

All banks	Median	0.34%	54.53%	26.15%	0.54%	61.79%	7.64%	0.99%	7.12%	8.77%
	Mean	1.17%	53.17%	26.08%	1.01%	58.22%	8.90%	2.70%	7.79%	11.85%
	Std dev.	2.37%	17.41%	12.44%	2.66%	20.71%	8.71%	3.96%	3.44%	10.25%
	P1.	0.00%	5.65%	0.08%	0.00%	2.79%	0.00%	0.00%	3.33%	0.72%
	P99.	11.84%	88.35%	64.12%	8.90%	90.96%	45.50%	18.98%	18.72%	47.46%
	Obs.	108,226	108,226	108,226	108,226	108,226	108,226	108,226	108,226	108,226

Source: Reproduced from Ayadi et al. (2017)

Notes: The independence of clusters (a.k.a. business models) with respect to each indicator was tested using Welch's two-sample tests at 5% significance. To report the results of these tests, the number of asterisks (*, **, and ***) stands for the statistical difference of any given cluster from that number of other clusters. For example, two asterisks (**) imply that the cluster is statistically different from two other clusters but not the third (closest) one. P1 and P99 are the 1st and 99th percentiles

Table C.3 Descriptive statistics for credit union business models, weighted

		Loans and deposits to/in credit unions and banks (% assets)	*Customer loans (% assets)*	*Trading assets (% assets)*	*Bank liabilities (% assets)*	*Customer deposits (% assets)*	*Derivative exposures (% assets)*	*Net worth (% assets)*	*Cash (% assets)*
Model 1—Retail type 1	Median	1.63%	70.59%	0.00%	0.00%	87.74%	0.00%	9.89%	6.40%
	Mean	3.91%**	71.35%**	0.12%**	1.96%**	86.83%*	0.02%*	10.24%**	7.57%**
	Std dev.	5.11%	8.64%	1.28%	3.11%	3.89%	0.52%	2.46%	5.05%
	P1	0.00%	56.45%	0.00%	0.00%	76.33%	0.00%	6.44%	0.98%
	P99	21.35%	89.36%	2.79%	10.96%	92.79%	0.00%	18.87%	24.55%
	Obs.	47,574	47,574	47,574	47,574	47,574	47,574	47,574	47,574
Model 2—Retail type 2	Median	2.04%	47.90%	0.00%	0.00%	87.46%	0.00%	10.78%	7.20%
	Mean	7.63%**	46.22%**	0.03%**	0.92%**	86.89%*	0.01%*	11.31%**	10.09%**
	Std dev.	9.89%	10.17%	0.65%	2.06%	3.64%	0.39%	3.08%	9.22%
	P1	0.00%	16.62%	0.00%	0.00%	75.28%	0.00%	6.98%	0.48%
	P99	33.97%	63.20%	0.10%	9.65%	92.38%	0.00%	22.65%	42.44%
	Obs.	41,655	41,655	41,655	41,655	41,655	41,655	41,655	41,610
Model 3—Retail type 3	Median	43.29%	37.92%	0.00%	0.00%	86.47%	0.00%	12.86%	7.13%
	Mean	45.13%**	36.9%**	0%**	0.19%**	85.53%**	0%**	13.77%**	8.61%**
	Std dev.	10.11%	10.13%	0.22%	0.94%	4.90%	0.00%	4.83%	6.53%
	P1	27.81%	11.31%	0.00%	0.00%	69.88%	0.00%	6.78%	0.39%
	P99	71.66%	54.71%	0.00%	4.65%	92.75%	0.00%	29.21%	31.80%
	Obs.	26,359	26,359	26,359	26,359	26,359	26,359	26,359	26,359
All credit unions	Median	2.11%	61.68%	0.00%	0.00%	87.60%	0.00%	10.25%	6.71%
	Mean	7.2%	60.3%	0.1%	1.5%	86.8%	0.02%	10.8%	8.6%
	Std dev.	11.42%	16.05%	1.05%	2.75%	3.86%	0.46%	2.97%	7.08%
	P1	0.00%	20.16%	0.00%	0.00%	75.79%	0.00%	6.57%	0.70%
	P99	53.12%	88.96%	1.26%	10.69%	92.62%	0.00%	22.01%	39.79%
	Obs.	115,588	115,588	115,588	115,588	115,588	115,588	115,588	115,588

Source: Reproduced from Ayadi et al. (2017)

Notes: The independence of clusters with respect to each indicator was tested using Welch's two-sample tests at 5% significance. To report the results of these tests, one asterisk (*) implies that the cluster is statistically different from one other cluster but not the third (closest) one. Two asterisks (**) mean that the cluster is statistically different from the other two clusters

Table C.4 Descriptive statistics for business models in Canada

		Bank loans (% assets)	*Customer loans (% assets)*	*Trading assets (% assets)*	*Bank liabilities (% assets)*	*Customer deposits (% assets)*	*Debt liabilities (% assets)*	*Derivative exposures (% assets)*	*Tang. Comm. eq. (%tang. Assets)*	*Cash (% assets)*
Model 1—Diversified Retail	Median	1.68%	50.43%	21.81%	0.41%	64.06%	0.00%	0.56%	3.83%	0.69%
	Mean	3.54%	51.49%	24.86%	3.04%	64.31%	0.22%	1.24%	4.00%	3.82%
	Std dev.	8.77%	7.19%	12.97%	4.74%	4.61%	3.08%	1.33%	1.19%	5.00%
	Min.	0.00%	0.00%	0.35%	0.00%	0.00%	0.00%	0.00%	−0.02%	0.00%
	Max.	95.03%	89.07%	54.58%	32.33%	89.93%	86.69%	5.50%	28.42%	14.97%
	Obs.	39	95	39	39	95	95	43	93	39
Model 2—Focused Retail	Median	0.00%	84.73%	9.88%	0.00%	85.17%	2.68%	0.02%	5.91%	0.97%
	Mean	3.91%	84.66%	9.31%	0.13%	84.61%	4.59%	0.08%	6.24%	1.32%
	Std dev.	5.63%	4.87%	4.66%	1.81%	8.04%	4.73%	0.21%	2.66%	1.52%
	Min.	0.00%	57.27%	0.61%	0.00%	52.88%	0.00%	0.00%	−0.12%	0.00%
	Max.	32.05%	95.64%	20.61%	32.68%	95.49%	30.38%	2.67%	20.23%	15.14%
	Obs.	164	196	162	155	196	196	179	191	164
Model 3—Investment oriented	Median	0.75%	12.84%	83.95%	0.00%	26.51%	13.86%	1.45%	8.17%	0.64%
	Mean	1.31%	12.71%	84.99%	3.71%	39.16%	27.71%	19.62%	9.62%	0.71%
	Std dev.	2.89%	5.23%	6.37%	6.38%	22.94%	23.99%	25.08%	7.78%	0.86%
	Min.	0.00%	0.00%	52.23%	0.00%	2.96%	0.00%	0.00%	4.25%	0.00%
	Max.	29.98%	31.46%	99.30%	32.12%	92.23%	70.77%	62.11%	74.98%	3.86%
	Obs.	29	30	29	29	30	30	30	30	29
All banks	Median	0.75%	50.92%	11.70%	0.00%	64.89%	0.00%	0.06%	3.83%	0.74%
	Mean	3.38%	52.52%	25.38%	1.16%	64.94%	0.60%	3.49%	4.14%	1.57%
	Std dev.	5.91%	10.23%	29.45%	3.85%	6.90%	4.53%	12.54%	1.59%	2.50%
	Min.	0.00%	0.00%	0.35%	0.00%	0.00%	0.00%	0.00%	−0.12%	0.00%
	Max.	95.03%	95.64%	99.30%	32.68%	95.49%	86.69%	62.11%	74.98%	15.14%
	Obs.	232	321	230	223	321	321	252	314	232

Source: Author

Notes: The independence of clusters was tested using non-parametric Wilcoxon-Mann-Witney two-sample tests at 5% significance. According to the results of these tests, the number of asterisks (* or **) stands for the statistical difference of any given cluster from that number of other clusters for that indicator. For example, two asterisks (**) implies that the cluster is statistically different from two other clusters but not the third and fourth (closest) ones

Table C.5 Descriptive statistics for ownership structures for banks in Europe

		Bank loans (% assets)	*Customer loans (% assets)*	*Trading assets (% assets)*	*Bank liabilities (% assets)*	*Customer deposits (% assets)*	*Debt liabilities (% assets)*	*Derivative exposures (% assets)*	*Tang. Comm. eq. (% tang. assets)*
Commercial	Mean	17.2%	48.8%	27.2%	15.1%	53.2%	17.6%	2.2%	11.2%
	Std dev.	0.206****	0.266****	0.222***	0.194***	0.277****	0.214****	0.072****	0.133****
	Min.	0.0%	0.0%	−87.7%	0.0%	0.0%	0.0%	0.0%	−233.3%
	Max.	100.0%	99.0%	100.0%	98.1%	101.4%	333.3%	90.8%	99.9%
	Obs	3814	3840	3735	3817	3817	3814	3861	3790
Cooperative	Mean	9.7%	63.0%	25.5%	12.9%	66.2%	13.7%	0.2%	6.8%
	Std dev.	0.09***	0.163****	0.142****	0.113***	0.19***	0.15***	0.011****	0.038***
	Min.	0.0%	0.0%	−6.8%	0.0%	0.0%	0.0%	0.0%	−2.2%
	Max.	100.0%	96.5%	98.0%	91.0%	98.3%	99.6%	22.0%	100.0%
	Obs	5315	5337	5290	5331	5331	5331	5358	5289
Nationalised	Mean	7.3%	57.6%	31.4%	16.2%	43.6%	32.1%	4.8%	1.7%
	Std dev.	0.061***	0.143****	0.129****	0.113****	0.208***	0.339***	0.084****	0.23****
	Min.	0.0%	11.8%	2.9%	0.0%	0.0%	2.0%	0.0%	−242.7%
	Max.	31.7%	86.7%	79.9%	61.2%	92.4%	342.7%	75.8%	22.7%
	Obs	270	270	270	268	268	268	271	253
Public	Mean	14.8%	62.2%	19.4%	14.5%	43.8%	30.8%	2.1%	8.9%
	Std dev.	0.199**	0.265****	0.173****	0.201***	0.304***	0.264***	0.036****	0.093****
	Min.	0.0%	0.1%	0.1%	0.0%	0.0%	0.1%	0.0%	0.4%
	Max.	96.7%	95.6%	97.2%	98.1%	91.4%	92.7%	18.5%	72.8%
	Obs	454	454	450	457	457	457	457	422

Savings	Mean	8.8%	64.3%	24.8%	12.7%	67.4%	12.1%	0.4%	7.2%
	Std dev.	0.087**	0.162****	0.132***	0.113***	0.162***	0.14***	0.018****	0.043***
	Min.	0.0%	0.0%	0.0%	0.0%	0.0%	0.0%	0.0%	−1.3%
	Max.	99.9%	99.2%	96.6%	94.8%	97.5%	99.3%	34.4%	94.2%
	Obs	3389	3427	3335	3402	3402	3400	3459	3370
All banks	Mean	11.8%	59.1%	25.7%	13.6%	61.5%	15.4%	1.0%	8.1%
	Std dev.	0.142	0.212	0.168	0.145	0.23	0.184	0.044	0.089
	Min.	0.0%	0.0%	−87.7%	0.0%	0.0%	0.0%	0.0%	−242.7%
	Max.	100.0%	99.2%	100.0%	98.1%	101.4%	342.7%	90.8%	100.0%
	Obs	13,242	13,328	13,080	13,275	13,275	13,270	13,406	13,124

Source: Reproduced from Ayadi et al. (2016)

Notes: The independence of the ownership structures was tested using non-parametric Wilcoxon-Mann-Witney two-sample tests at 5% significance. According to the results of these tests, the number of asterisks (*, **, ***, and ****) stands for the statistical difference of any given ownership structure from that number of other ownership structures for that indicator. For example, two asterisks (**) implies that the ownership structures is statistically different from two other ownership structures but not the third and fourth (closest) ones

Table C.6 Descriptive statistics for bank size categories in the US, weighted

		Loans to banks (% assets)	*Customer loans (% assets)*	*Trading assets (% assets)*	*Bank liabilities (% assets)*	*Customer deposits (% assets)*	*Debt liabilities (% assets)*	*Derivative exposures (% assets)*	*Tangible. Common equity (% tangible. assets)*	*Cash (% assets)*
Micro	Median	0.00%	66.30%	19.70%	0.01%	82.86%	2.79%	0.00%	9.07%	6.05%
(<1 bn)	Mean	0.1%****	63.81%***	22.26%**	1.5%****	80.25%****	4.89%****	0.01%****	10.02%****	8.39%**
	Std dev.	1.65%	15.48%	14.60%	5.50%	11.66%	6.29%	0.17%	5.43%	8.33%
	P1.	0.00%	0.00%	0.00%	0.00%	0.00%	0.00%	0.00%	0.00%	1.01%
	P99.	98.77%	98.77%	99.80%	94.00%	100.00%	89.17%	11.30%	100.00%	40.71%
	Obs.	100,430	100,430	100,430	100,430	100,430	100,430	100,430	100,430	100,430
Very small	Median	0.00%	66.16%	19.85%	0.05%	78.42%	4.68%	0.00%	8.57%	4.30%
(1–5 bn)	Mean	0.16%****	63.34%***	22.51%*	1.01%**	74.15%****	7.22%****	0.03%****	9.52%***	7.31%**
	Std dev.	1.29%	16.13%	14.23%	3.78%	16.51%	9.19%	0.15%	5.15%	10.03%
	P1.	0.00%	0.00%	0.00%	0.00%	0.00%	0.00%	0.00%	0.66%	0.50%
	P99.	30.09%	99.24%	97.35%	64.06%	94.71%	95.80%	3.54%	91.80%	52.48%
	Obs.	5628	5628	5628	5628	5628.00	5628	5628	5628	5628
Small	Median	0.00%	63.55%	21.40%	0.05%	71.83%	7.03%	0.00%	8.14%	3.87%
(5–10 bn)	Mean	0.51%***	60.54%***	24.02%**	0.74%***	65.67%****	10.89%***	0.11%****	9.26%***	7.96%*
	Std dev.	2.99%	17.40%	16.45%	2.04%	20.91%	14.62%	0.39%	4.40%	11.97%
	P1.	0.00%	0.00%	0.00%	0.00%	0.00%	0.00%	0.00%	0.72%	0.26%
	P99.	53.30%	97.20%	98.58%	23.60%	93.80%	88.35%	7.37%	40.96%	78.81%
	Obs.	854	854	854	854	854	854	854	854	854

Mid-sized	Median	0.00%	63.68%	20.94%	0.16%	68.01%	9.27%	0.05%	7.52%	4.60%
(10–50 bn)	Mean	0.63%***	60.36%***	23.21%*	0.92%*	62.69%****	12.54%***	0.35%****	8.21%****	8.15%*
	Std dev.	2.73%	17.93%	16.10%	3.68%	20.73%	14.75%	0.80%	3.08%	9.38%
	P1.	0.00%	0.05%	0.00%	0.00%	0.00%	0.00%	0.00%	0.36%	0.12%
	P99.	50.49%	98.06%	98.84%	78.67%	94.56%	93.53%	6.94%	25.46%	42.80%
	Obs.	908	908	908	908	908	908	908	908	908
Large	Median	1.04%	50.61%	27.75%	0.84%	52.33%	7.95%	2.78%	6.60%	11.00%
(>50 bn)	Mean	1.6%****	48.4%****	27.8%****	0.96%**	51.33%****	9%****	4.06%****	7.04%****	13.87%****
	Std dev.	2.34%	15.76%	10.21%	1.04%	18.15%	6.39%	4.30%	2.28%	10.05%
	P1.	0.00%	2.58%	0.00%	0.00%	0.11%	0.00%	0.00%	1.56%	1.51%
	P99.	30.10%	93.60%	79.96%	25.06%	93.15%	77.07%	40.64%	20.73%	47.46%
	Obs.	406	406	406	406	406	406	406	406	406
All banks	Median	0.34%	54.53%	26.15%	0.54%	61.79%	7.64%	0.99%	7.12%	8.77%
	Mean	1.17%	53.17%	26.08%	1.01%	58.22%	8.90%	2.70%	7.80%	11.85%
	Std dev.	2.37%	17.41%	12.44%	2.66%	20.71%	8.71%	3.96%	3.41%	10.25%
	P1.	0.00%	5.65%	0.08%	0.00%	2.79%	0.00%	0.00%	3.33%	0.72%
	P99.	11.84%	88.35%	64.12%	8.90%	90.96%	45.50%	18.98%	18.75%	47.46%
	Obs.	108,226	108,226	108,226	108,226	108,226	108,226	108,226	108,226	108,226

Source: Reproduced from Ayadi et al. (2017)

Notes: The independence of bank size categories with respect to each indicator was tested using Welch two-sample tests at 5% significance. To report the results of these tests, the number of asterisks (*, **, ***, and ****) stands for the statistical difference of any given size category from that number of other size categories. For example, two asterisks (**) imply that the size category is statistically different from two other size categories but not the third and fourth (closest) ones. P1 and P99 are the 1st and 99th percentiles

Table C.7 Descriptive statistics for institution type in Canada

		Bank loans (% assets)	*Customer loans (% assets)*	*Trading assets (% assets)*	*Bank liabilities (% assets)*	*Customer deposits (% assets)*	*Debt liabilities (% assets)*	*Derivative exposures (% assets)*	*Tang. Comm. eq. (% tang. Assets)*	*Cash (% assets)*
Local banks and Desjardins group	Median	9.40%	50.43%	1.89%	0.00%	64.89%	0.00%	0.00%	3.83%	0.00%
	Mean	13.44%	51.76%	2.30%	0.01%	64.75%	0.04%	0.01%	3.97%	0.09%
	Std dev.	5.99%	7.93%	0.80%	0.28%	4.83%	0.61%	0.02%	0.94%	0.15%
	Min.	8.61%	37.59%	1.01%	0.00%	51.28%	0.00%	0.00%	−0.12%	0.00%
	Max.	32.05%	95.15%	3.44%	5.75%	93.13%	10.35%	0.08%	10.03%	0.97%
	Obs.	9	75	9	12	75	75	12	70	9
Foreign banks	Median	2.60%	58.29%	24.09%	2.76%	59.88%	0.00%	1.37%	4.98%	0.05%
	Mean	5.08%	54.97%	38.90%	5.12%	55.84%	5.97%	15.24%	7.04%	2.29%
	Std dev.	8.02%	17.25%	30.31%	6.73%	15.68%	13.59%	23.18%	5.98%	4.34%
	Min.	0.11%	0.00%	0.35%	0.00%	0.00%	0.00%	0.00%	−0.02%	0.00%
	Max.	95.03%	91.78%	99.30%	32.68%	92.23%	86.69%	62.11%	74.98%	14.97%
	Obs.	81	92	81	75	92	92	86	92	81
Credit unions	Median	0.00%	84.73%	10.62%	0.00%	86.63%	6.76%	0.05%	5.87%	1.05%
	Mean	1.97%	74.29%	22.70%	0.00%	80.16%	12.76%	0.20%	6.12%	1.45%
	Std dev.	3.69%	27.03%	28.44%	0.00%	17.16%	17.36%	0.37%	1.91%	1.45%
	Min.	0.00%	1.51%	1.27%	0.00%	21.74%	0.00%	0.00%	2.72%	0.06%
	Max.	15.89%	95.64%	96.94%	0.00%	95.49%	70.77%	1.53%	16.74%	15.14%
	Obs.	142	154	140	136	154	154	154	152	142
All banks	Median	0.75%	50.92%	11.70%	0.00%	64.89%	0.00%	0.06%	3.83%	0.74%
	Mean	3.38%	52.52%	25.38%	1.16%	64.94%	0.60%	3.49%	4.14%	1.57%
	Std dev.	5.91%	10.23%	29.45%	3.85%	6.90%	4.53%	12.54%	1.59%	2.50%
	Min.	0.00%	0.00%	0.35%	0.00%	0.00%	0.00%	0.00%	−0.12%	0.00%
	Max.	95.03%	95.64%	99.30%	32.68%	95.49%	86.69%	62.11%	74.98%	15.14%
	Obs.	232	321	230	223	321	321	252	314	232

Source: Author

Notes: The independence of the ownership structures was tested using non-parametric Wilcoxon-Mann-Witney two-sample tests at 5% significance. According to the results of these tests, the number of asterisks (*, ** and ***) stands for the statistical difference of any given ownership structure from that number of other ownership structures for that indicator. For example, two asterisks (**) implies that the ownership structures is statistically different from two other ownership structures but not the third and fourth (closest) ones

Appendix D: Descriptive Statistics for BBM Assessment

Table D.1 Description of indicators in Europe

Variable	*Coverage (%)*	*Mean*	*Std dev.*	*Min.*	*Max.*
(Financial) Activities					
Loans to banks (% of assets)	99	0.118	0.142	0.000	1.000
Customer loans (% of assets)	99	0.591	0.212	0.000	0.992
Trading assets (% of assets)	98	0.257	0.167	0.000	1.000
Bank liabilities (% of assets)	99	0.136	0.145	0.000	0.981
Customer deposits (% of assets)	99	0.615	0.230	0.000	1.014
Debt liabilities (% of assets)	99	0.154	0.184	0.000	3.427
Derivative exposure (% of assets)	100	0.010	0.044	0.000	0.908
Tang. comm. eq. (% tang. assets)	98	0.081	0.089	−2.427	1.000
(International) Activities					
No. of unique EEA countries	98	1.553	2.166	1.000	22.000
No. of unique EEA countries through subsidiaries	98	0.257	1.227	0.000	16.000
No. of unique EEA countries through branches	98	0.295	1.189	0.000	12.000
Ownership					
Shareholder value (dummy var.)	100	0.308	0.462	0.000	1.000
Commercial (dummy var.)	100	0.288	0.453	0.000	1.000
Nationalised (dummy var.)	100	0.020	0.141	0.000	1.000
Stakeholder value (dummy var.)	100	0.692	0.462	0.000	1.000
Cooperative (dummy var.)	100	0.400	0.490	0.000	1.000

(*continued*)

R. Ayadi, *Banking Business Models*, Palgrave Macmillan Studies in Banking and Financial Institutions,
https://doi.org/10.1007/978-3-030-02248-8

Table D.1 (continued)

Variable	*Coverage (%)*	*Mean*	*Std dev.*	*Min.*	*Max.*
Savings (dummy var.)	100	0.258	0.438	0.000	1.000
Public (dummy var.)	100	0.034	0.181	0.000	1.000
Listed on stock exchange (dummy var.)	100	0.121	0.326	0.000	1.000
Financial performance					
Return on assets (RoA)	99	0.004	0.044	−2.215	1.933
Return on equity (RoE)	99	0.042	1.457	−104.545	53.040
Cost-to-income ratio (CIR)	99	0.723	3.356	−40.810	350.782
Net interest income (% of total income)	99	0.694	2.074	−18.788	226.188
Trading income (% of total income)	96	0.015	2.236	−227.313	24.478
Commission & fee income (% of total income)	99	0.219	0.268	−5.468	11.562
Other income (% of total income)	96	0.072	0.529	−24.859	39.385
Customer loan growth (% change)	80	5.531	413.734	−1.000	41154.9
Riskiness					
Z-score (no. of std dev. from default)	97	69.790	98.380	−12.145	1786.205
Loan loss provisions (% of gross customer loans)	53	0.013	0.166	−1.067	11.634
Stock returns (avg. daily returns)	11	0.000	0.003	−0.011	0.067
Stock returns (std dev. daily returns)	11	0.026	0.0233	0.000	0.421
CDS spread (senior annual avg.)	6	1.765	2.110	0.046	18.363
CDS spread (senior annual std dev.)	6	0.433	0.619	0	4.655
Government exposure (% of own funds)	0.9	2.352	3.558	−5.677	31.734
Home country exposure (% of government exp.)	0.9	0.732	0.290	0.000	1.000
Regulation					
Risk-weighted assets (RWA) (% of assets)	79	1.046	14.991	0.000	721.687
Tier 1 capital ratio (% of risk-weighted assets)	70	0.149	0.141	−0.165	4.739
AQR 2014/15 impact (% of RWA)	0.9	−0.006	0.008	−0.039	0.002
Stress test 2014/15 impact (% of RWA)	0.9	0.008	0.194	−0.152	0.962
Shortfall (% of RWA)	0.9	0.008	0.022	0.000	0.135
Tangible common equity (% tang. assets)	99	0.082	0.078	−0.129	1.000
Cumulative peak losses aided banks (% of total liabilities aided banks)[a]	2.5	0.067	0.082	0.000	0.345

Source: Reproduced from Ayadi et al. (2016)

[a]The cumulative peak losses cover multiple years; the coverage is, therefore, calculated as share of total number of banks instead of bank-year observations

Table D.2 Description of indicators for banks in the US

Variable	*Median*	*Mean*	*Std dev.*	*P1.*	*P99.*	*Completeness (%)*
Financial performance						
Return on assets (ROA, in %)	1.24	1.28	2.00	2.00	5.53	100
Return on equity (ROE, in %)	12.42	12.31	14.13	14.13	48.36	100
Cost-to-income ratio (CIR, in %)	60.23	61.26	17.35	17.35	106.74	100
Net interest income (% of operating income)	60.11	60.39	19.02	19.02	97.72	100
Trading income (% of operating income)	20.85	24.07	19.12	19.12	89.80	100
Commission & fee income (% of operating income)	0.11	0.40	6.64	6.64	7.66	100
Other income (% of operating income)	13.32	15.88	12.53	12.53	70.24	92
Customer loan growth (% change)	3.99	4.42	12.08	12.08	39.60	86
Riskiness						
Z-score (no. of std dev. from default)	19.03	20.04	12.78	2.51	66.59	97
Loan loss provisions (% of gross customer loans)	0.53	0.53	2.05	2.05	7.02	100
Stock returns (average daily returns, in %)	0.06	0.06	1.66	1.66	4.15	18
Stock returns (standard deviations of daily returns, in %)	2.29	2.29	5.89	5.89	22.86	18
Regulatory capital						
Risk-weighted assets (RWA) (% of assets)	71.94	72.19	15.09	32.40	114.17	100
Tier 1 capital (% of risk-weighted assets)	10.20	11.15	6.67	6.46	28.07	100
Total capital (% of risk-weighted assets)	12.93	14.46	61.53	10.13	35.53	100
Tangible common equity (% tangible assets)	7.12	7.80	3.41	3.33	18.75	100
NSFR (available/required funding, in %)	129.42	150.25	1405.27	92.71	251.64	92

Source: Reproduced from Ayadi et al. (2017)

Note: P1 and P99 are the 1st and 99th percentiles

Table D.3 Description of indicators for credit unions in the US

Variable	*Median*	*Mean*	*Std dev.*	*P1.*	*P99.*	*Completeness (%)*
Financial performance						
Return on assets (RoA, in %)	0.74	0.68	6.58	−1.69	1.97	100.00
Return on equity (RoE, in %)	6.66	6.02	10.17	−17.24	18.10	99.99
Cost-to-income ratio (CIR, in %)	74.00	73.80	13.09	40.43	106.21	99.94
Net interest income (% of gross income)	54.17	54.15	9.92	32.23	78.02	99.98
Trading income (% of gross income)	0.00	0.01	0.36	−0.04	0.25	99.98
Commission & fee income (% of gross income)	12.50	13.67	7.96	0.49	37.85	99.86
Other income (% of gross income)	7.60	8.51	6.78	0.00	28.05	99.98
Customer loan growth (% change)	6.31	6.48	9.92	−17.59	32.81	98.69
Riskiness						
Z-score (no. of std dev. from default)	27.29	30.04	16.94	5.54	86.33	98.02
Loan loss provisions (% Gross loans)	0.48	0.68	0.83	−0.26	3.87	99.91
Regulatory capital						
Net worth ratio (% of assets)	10.24	10.83	2.96	6.70	22.04	100
Risk-based net worth requirements (% of assets)	6.51	6.74	0.79	6.01	9.97	5.52

Source: Reproduced from Ayadi et al. (2017)

Note: P1 and P99 are the 1st and 99th percentiles

Table D.4 Description of indicators used for banks and credit unions in Canada

Variable	*Coverage*	*Median*	*Mean*	*Std dev.*		*Min*	*Max*
Financial activities							
Loans to banks (% of assets)	72.27%	0.75%	3.38%	5.91%		0.00%	95.03%
Customer loans (% of assets)	100.00%	50.92%	52.52%	10.23%		0.00%	95.64%
Trading assets (% of assets)	71.65%	11.70%	25.38%	29.45%		0.35%	99.30%
Bank liabilities (% of assets)	69.47%	0.00%	1.16%	3.85%		0.00%	32.68%
Customer deposits (% of assets)	100.00%	64.89%	64.94%	6.90%		0.00%	95.49%
Debt liabilities (% of assets)	100.00%	0.00%	0.63%	4.81%		0.00%	86.69%
Derivative exposure (% of assets)	78.50%	0.06%	3.49%	12.54%		0.00%	62.11%
Tang. comm. eq. (% of tang. assets)	97.82%	3.83%	4.14%	1.59%		−0.12%	74.98%
Financial performance							
Return on assets (RoA)	99.07%	1.00%	1.02%	0.18%	−2.02%	2.41%	
Return on equity (RoE)	99.07%	17.85%	17.50%	4.12%	−47.34%	24.96%	
Cost-to-income ratio (CIR)	98.75%	62.17%	63.15%	8.05%	20.02%	219.72%	
Net interest income (% of operating income)	98.75%	53.01%	50.39%	10.57%	9.97%	381.15%	
Trading income (% of operating income)	91.59%	5.88%	5.88%	4.32%	−377.23%	162.30%	
Commission & fee income (% of operating income)	80.69%	23.17%	23.63%	4.65%	−5.87%	96.90%	
Other income (% of operating income)	98.75%	19.25%	29.14%	19.10%	−277.02%	96.07%	
Customer loan growth (% change)	79.44%	0.76%	4.95%	12.94%	−78.89%	217.42%	
Riskiness							
Z-score (no. of std dev. from default)	94.70%	98.510	126.742	58.187	3.219	243.234	
Loan loss provisions (% of gross customer loans)	85.05%	0.33%	0.33%	0.13%	−2.42%	4.22%	
Stock returns (avg. daily returns)	17.76%	0.05%	0.02%	0.10%	−0.39%	0.19%	
Stock returns (std dev. daily returns)	17.76%	1.14%	1.55%	1.47%	0.64%	8.16%	
Regulatory capital							
Risk-weighted assets (RWA) (% of assets)	77.57%	37.10%	36.93%	7.35%	2.80%	143.70%	
Tier 1 capital (% of risk-weighted assets)	67.29%	12.20%	12.66%	4.23%	9.04%	601.05%	
Total capital (% of risk-weighted assets)	77.26%	14.43%	15.09%	4.14%	8.69%	601.05%	
Tangible common equity (% tang. assets)	97.82%	3.83%	4.14%	1.59%	−0.12%	74.98%	
NSFR(avail./req. funding)	100.00%	117.22%	116.11%	8.98%	49.39%	2232.85%	

Source: Author

Appendix E: The Computation of the Z-Score

The Z-score used follows the one derived in Boyd and Runkle (1993), which is a simple indicator of the risk of failure or the distance to default. To derive the measure, it is assumed that default occurs when the one-time losses of bank j in year t exceed its equity, or when

$$\pi_{jt} + E_{jt} < 0 \tag{E.1}$$

Then, assuming that the bank's return on total assets (ROA), or π_{jt}/TA_{jt}, is normally distributed around the mean μ_j, and standard deviation σ_j, the probability of failure is given as

$$pr\left(\pi_{jt} < -E_{jt}\right) = pr\left(\pi_{jt} / TA_{jt} < -E_{jt} / TA_{jt}\right) = \int_{-\infty}^{D_{jt}} \phi\left(r\right) dr \tag{E.2}$$

where ϕ represents the standard normal distribution, r is the standardised return on assets and D is the default boundary that separates a healthy bank from an unhealthy one, described as the normalised equity ratio:

$$D_{jt} = \frac{-\left(E_{jt} / TA_{jt}\right) - \mu_j}{\sigma_j} \tag{E.3}$$

R. Ayadi, *Banking Business Models*, Palgrave Macmillan Studies in Banking and Financial Institutions,
https://doi.org/10.1007/978-3-030-02248-8

Note that a greater D implies a greater probability of default and, therefore, a greater risk for the bank. The average and standard deviation calculations were obtained using available data in the samples.

Since D admits negative values in most cases, the Z-score is set to be represented as a positive number, or as

$$Z_{jt} = -D_{jt} \tag{E.4}$$

This implies that a greater Z-value implies a lower probability of default.

Appendix F: Credit Unions Regulation in the US

Prompt Corrective Action Capital Guidelines for US Credit Unions

For US credit unions, the Prompt Correct Action (PCA) framework is coded in the Credit Union Membership Access Act (CUMAA) of 1998. The requirements in the table below are those that were binding over the period 2000–2014. The only provision that changed is the definition of complex credit union, raising the total asset threshold in 2013 from $10 mn to $50 mn.

Table F.1 Prompt corrective action threshold for credit unions

Classification	*Net worth ratio*		*And subject to*
Well capitalised	7% or above	AND	If complex, meet applicable RBNW requirements
Adequately capitalised	6%–6.99%	AND	If complex, meet applicable RBNW requirements
Undercapitalised	4%–5.99%	OR	If complex, fails applicable RBNW requirement
Significantly undercapitalised	2%–3.99%	OR	if undercapitalised at 0–5% net worth ratio and fails to timely submit or materially implement net worth restoration plan
Critically undercapitalised	0%–2%		None

Source: Code of Federal regulations, Title 12, 702.10

R. Ayadi, *Banking Business Models*, Palgrave Macmillan Studies in Banking and Financial Institutions,
https://doi.org/10.1007/978-3-030-02248-8

Note that, in 2015, the NCUA has redesigned this framework into a risk-based capital (RBC) system that more closely mimics bank risk-based capital requirements. The new RBC will become binding in 2019.

Appendix G: The Computation of NSFR

The assumptions for the **net stable funding ratio** (NSFR) are similar to those put forward in IMF (2011). Introduced by the Basel Committee on Banking Supervision (BCBS 2010), the NSFR aims to restrict banks from having an excessive reliance on short-term funding, in an attempt to promote more balanced, mid-to-long-term financial resources, in order to support assets through stable funding sources. More specifically, the measure requires the available stable funding to exceed the required stable funding.

Available stable funding sources include total Tier 1 and Tier 2 capital, as well as reserves that count as part of equity. Stable forms of funding, including customer deposits and other liabilities with more than one-year maturities, are also included. Lower maturity liabilities, including term deposits and retail deposits from non-financial institutions, enter as available funding after the application of various haircuts. Short-term liabilities to financial institutions and secured wholesale funding are generally not included as available, due to substantial rollover risks and potential margin calls that may materialise in times of market stress.

Required stable funding includes assets that cannot be quickly sold off without substantial costs during adverse market conditions, lasting up to one year. Most customer loans are assumed to have long-term maturities and will, thus, face liquidation costs. All encumbered securities that are posted as collateral enter directly into the calculation of required stable funding, as they cannot be sold off without changing the original contract. Shorter maturity retail loans are also treated as required funding, albeit

R. Ayadi, *Banking Business Models*, Palgrave Macmillan Studies in Banking and Financial Institutions,
https://doi.org/10.1007/978-3-030-02248-8

with an appropriate haircut. In turn, more liquid unencumbered assets, such as cash or marketable securities, receive lower factors, as they are, typically, readily available for sale without substantial potential losses.

Since the available data is quite restricted in nature, assumptions regarding many specific items were made. The following table provides the assumptions and the relevant multiplicative factors that were used to build the NSFR measure used in this study. Although comparable to the measure developed by IMF (2011), the validity of the results is likely to depend on the assumptions for certain factors more than on those for others. This is particularly the case for debt liabilities and trading assets, which make up more than one-third of the balance sheets of most banks, especially in the investment and wholesale banking models.

Balance sheet items			
Available stable funding	*Factors (%)*	*Required stable funding*	*Factors (%)*
Customer deposits	85	Cash	0
Deposits from banks	0	Customer loans	80
Derivative liabilities (negative, fair value)	0	Loans to banks	0
Debt liabilities	50	Derivative assets (positive, fair value)	90
Equity & reserves	100	Trading assets	50

Source: Reproduced from Ayadi et al. (2012)

References

Ayadi, R., E. Arbak and W.P. de Groen (2012), *Regulation of European Banks and Business Models: Towards a new paradigm?* Centre for European Policy Studies (CEPS), Brussels.

Ayadi, R., W.P. de Groen, Sassi, I., Mathlouthi, W., Rey, H. and Aubry O. (2016), "Banking Business Models Monitor 2015 EUROPE", Montreal, International Research Centre on Cooperative Finance (IRCCF) publication (http://finance-coop.hec.ca/publications/etudes/banking-business-models-monitor-2015-europe-rym-ayadi/).

Ayadi, R. et al. (2017), "Bank and Credit Unions Business Models in the United States", Montreal, International Research Centre On Cooperative Finance, HEC Montreal.

BCBS (2010), "Basel III: International framework for liquidity risk measurement, standards and monitoring", Basel Committee on Banking Supervision, Bank for International Settlements, Basel, December.

Boyd, J.H. and D.E. Runkle (1993), "Size and Performance of Banking Firms: Testing the Predictions of Theory", *Journal of Monetary Economics*, Vol. 31, No. 1, pp. 47–67.

IMF (2011), "Global Financial Stability Report: Durable Financial Stability: Getting There from Here", International Monetary Fund, Washington, DC.

Index

R. Ayadi, *Banking Business Models*, Palgrave Macmillan Studies in Banking and Financial Institutions,
https://doi.org/10.1007/978-3-030-02248-8

The manufacturer's authorised representative in the EU is Springer Nature Customer Service Centre GmbH, Europaplatz 3, 69115 Heidelberg, Germany. If you have any concerns regarding our products, please contact ProductSafety@springernature.com

Printed and bound by CPI Group (UK) Ltd, Croydon, CR0 4YY
22/09/2026
02221067-0002